FAITH FATIGUE

And What To Do About It

Other Books by Robert R. Leichtman, M.D.

Psychic Vandalism
The Psychic Life
The Curse of Fundamentalism
Recovering From Death and Other Disasters
Fear No Evil
The Psychic Perspective
The Inner Side of Life
The Hidden Side of Science
The Priests of God
The Dynamics of Creativity
The Destiny of America

with Carl Japikse:

Active Meditation
Forces of the Zodiac
The Art of Living
The Life of Spirit
I Ching On Line
Brainwashed!
The Light of Learning
The Revelation of Light
The Lights of Heaven
Embracing the Light

FAITH FATIGUE

And What To Do About It

by Robert R. Leichtman, M.D.

ENTHEA PRESS
Atlanta, Georgia

FAITH FATIGUE
Copyright © 2001 by Robert Leichtman, M.D.

All Rights Reserved. No part of this book may be used or reproduced in any manner whatsoever without written permission, except in the case of brief quotations embodied in articles and reviews. Printed in the United States of America. Direct inquiries to Enthea Press, P.O. Box 251, Marble Hill, GA 30148.

ISBN 0-89804-851-6

Contents

	Introduction	7
	Part I: The Role of Faith	11
1	What is Faith All About?	12
2	What is Faith Fatigue?	24
3	How Faith Works	35
4	How Faith Can Work Against Us	51
5	The Basis of Healing Faith Fatigue	68
	Part II: Healing the Faith Killers	73
6	Healing Doubt and Hesitation	74
7	Healing Ignorance	84
8	Healing Laziness	98
9	Healing Rationalization	110
	Part III: Cultivating Faith Builders	119
10	Tools of Faith Building	121
11	Faith in People	131
12	Faith in Our Experiences	146
13	Faith in Divine Opportunity	160
	Conclusion	170

Introduction

Faith is the linchpin of our daily activities. No matter whether we are heading for success or for disaster, it is faith that holds together our hopes or fears. Faith is the catalyst that magnifies our most basic attitudes about ourselves. When we believe in constructive possibilities, our faith can be a channel for healing, renewal, and growth. When we believe in the dark potential of failure or hardship, our faith can be an agent of doom, destruction, and defeat. Faith is the tool we can use to create either a heaven or hell on earth for us. It all depends on how wisely we use it.

Faith fuels our aliveness and vitality. When it is present in large amounts, it can fill us with hope, courage, enthusiasm, and ambition. When our faith is exhausted, however, we are reduced to barely surviving. The zest in our life seems gone. This is faith fatigue.

Faith fatigue results in a personal dissipation of strength, courage, and hope. The mental territory in which we travel shrinks to bland and familiar roads that seem safe and free of conflict. We lose the curiosity to explore new ideas and possibilities. We surrender the courage to risk change. We abandon the endurance to take on major challenges. Even worse, we become vulnerable to defeat by minor mistakes, criticism, and setbacks, because we lack the strength to drive through these challenges.

Faith fatigue exhausts us of our ability to dream of new possibilities, to risk change, and to revise the direction of our life. The net result is that we quietly and gradually surrender the control of our life to old habits, beliefs, and thinking that seems safe and comfortable to us. And in that safety, we begin to die—not in the body but in our imagination and curiosity, in our ambition and initiative. Later, this fatigue begins to kill off our endurance and patience; we expect less, do less, and achieve less. Still later, faith fatigue kills off our peace of mind and confidence, so we become more protective of our vulnerabilities and weaknesses. Slowly, our humanity shrinks to the tiny dimensions of our limitations, fears, and regrets.

Faith fatigue is not recognized by the counseling professions as a separate disease or malady. However, it is the subtext or background to a multitude of personal problems. It is a phenomenon that deserves our closest scrutiny and strongest efforts to overcome it.

This book divides the problem of faith fatigue into three parts. The first describes the basic nature and dynamic activities of faith. This section examines how our faith works for or against our welfare. It outlines what faith can and cannot do, the mechanics of how faith works, and how we often unwittingly use faith to harm ourself. It concludes by decribing the paradigm we need for change and healing.

The second part exposes faith killers, describing the four major habits that can sabotage our faith. These enemies are the habits of doubt, ignorance, laziness, and rationalization. If we are to heal faith fatigue, we must learn about the nature of the enemies of faith and how to neutralize them.

The third section explores faith building: how to generate the basic qualities we need to maintain faith in ourself and our relationships. In this part, the topic of faith is treated as a means to health and success rather than an end in itself. Faith is placed in the context of our relationship to real life situations. Here we must learn how to use faith to sustain alliances with the constructive elements of other people, our experiences, and higher powers and possibilities.

—Robert R. Leichtman, M.D.

Part One:
THE ROLE OF FAITH

chapter 1

What is Faith All About?

Before we can consider how to heal faith fatigue, we must acquire a good working knowledge of what faith is, what it is not, and how it works. While many people assume they have a sophisticated understanding of faith, most of them do not, and they suffer greatly because of it.

A critical lack of faith is exposed when we find ourself hesitant in times of crisis, doubtful in times of decision, and cautious in times of hardship. These are the types of events in which we are likely to experience a significant fatigue of our faith. Thereafter, our confidence and assertiveness can decrease to a hazardous level, endangering our success, health, and happiness.

Our first line defense for maintaining productive faith in ourself is knowledge of what genuine faith is and how it works.

Imposter Types of Faith

The most tragic mistake that we can make about faith is failing to realize that we have been working with impostors of faith, not the real thing. Just as counterfeit money can not be used to purchase goods, imposter faith can not be used to obtain what we want.

The major imposter of genuine faith is *wishing*. Embarrassing as it can be, far too many devout believers in God and divine potentials merely wish for what they want. They are only exercising a strong desire for something and then presuming this is all there is to faith. The fatal flaw in wishing is that most or all of our attention is focused on getting the benefits of what we want. This kind of faith omits any attention or devotion to a higher authority that has the power to cause what we want to occur. Wishing is an activity that involves only our personality and its preferences. It has only the limited power of emotional magnetism. It may draw to us people and situations that are similar to our state of mind and attitude, but is unlikely to bring into play the higher powers essential for major changes and accomplishments. Wishing is a feeble substitute for real faith. It will fail us in times of genuine need.

Imposter faith is also contrived out of *denial and arrogance*. People who are offended by certain facts and events often try to impose an egotistical bravado on reality. They presume that they can intimidate reality into submission by focusing all of their attention and energy on what they want and their right to obtain it. Their faulty assumption is that their whim and strong will are the supreme authorities in their personal world. Thereafter, they confidently ignore the real forces and activities about them. A strong will, intelligently directed, is a genuine asset and also a spiritual virtue. However, it is not a good substitute for faith, because denial and arrogance leave out any significant attention to forces greater than our personality and body. Genuine faith will always include the power of our personal strengths *within* the authority of higher intelligence and forces in the world. In times of crises, arrogance and denial are doomed to die a painful death from the many blows that reality will inevitably give them.

The most popular imposter of faith is *surrender,* the naïve, passive state in which we assume whatever we want will just come to us if we are sufficiently patient. Our general, vague belief in all good things is supposed to work magic by "allowing our highest good to find us" when we stop resisting it. This may work for those who want to get wet while standing in the rain, but it does not accomplish much else.

The mystery of why passive naïveté is so popular is probably due to the fact that it requires neither effort nor sacrifice. While indolence is a continual temptation for many, it is obvious that the gentle, passive state is just another disguise for emptiness. This is usually a very undesirable state, because it allows external events and many internal forces to reign unchecked.

The reputation of the gentle, passive state also derives from the fact that it is a step forward for a small group of people who are continually upset about something and habitually complain about it. By their endless annoyance—especially about situations they cannot change—they continually agitate themselves and others. The effort to become quiet and empty can lead to tremendous improvements in their mood and concentration, solely because they stop getting in the way of their serenity.

For the rest of us, however, the "activity" of being gentle and passive is just another way to avoid making the changes and doing the things that will foster success in our life. It is based on the simplistic belief that we will enjoy good luck and get what we want just by patient waiting. It is the most seductive imposter of genuine faith.

What is faith then?

In general, faith is belief in the presence and authority of something. We might, for instance, believe in the power of a tumor to kill us or the value of a friend to help us in a time of crisis. We could also believe in a plan that will boost our career, a new technique that will make our domestic activities more efficient, or in our ability to communicate more effectively with our children.

We can believe in all kinds of intangible things and abstract forces that we do not see. For instance, we can believe in the power of gravity, the principles of mathematics, and the laws of mechanical forces. Or, at a more subtle level, we can believe in the cosmic principles of justice and divine order.

Obviously, we can believe in things that do not exist—either in actuality or as a potential. Even then, our own belief will have the power to influence us. For instance, we can believe that we are endowed with superhuman strengths and talents that we do not genuinely have. This may give us unusual confidence that stimulates the very best in us and, in turn, aids us in achieving an extraordinary personal performance not otherwise possible.

Psychology would define faith as an emotional belief or attitude about people, situations, objects, or ourself. It can be linked to what is real and tangible or the potential inherent in any thing. These beliefs can be positive or negative. For instance, we can believe in the dishonesty of one person, or the incompetence of another. Or we might believe in the risk of a plan or the weakness of a method. We might be enthusiastic about our work or disgusted with our in-laws. We can doubt certain possibilities and believe in others.

The crucial factor about faith is that our faith in any of these attributes or possibilities defines our relationship to them and how they will influence us.

This means anxious people who have sustained faith in threats to their well-being will see themselves in danger and act to avoid these threats or defend themselves. Angry people who have strong faith in the harm done to them by others will stay hostile and act to retaliate or defend themselves. Sad people who believe their situation is hopeless will resign themselves to enduring what they dislike.

Cheerful people who have faith in the value of who they are and what they are doing will see opportunity and good potential everywhere and will prepare themselves to be involved with them. Patient and tolerant people have faith in the correctness of their vision of what situations mean and the innate good potential everywhere. They will act with moderation and self-control.

The quality and focus of our faith can be a powerful factor in determining how well we utilize all of our opportunities and strengths as well as how much we sabotage ourselves.

Naturally, ordinary faith can be applied to mundane aspects of life as well as the inner side of life and the creative divine forces that surround us. And just as naturally, our faith in the subtle, invisible forces around us can be positive or negative. That is, we can fear or love God. We can dread or enthusiastically embrace our destiny. We can doubt or accept the presence of the power of divine order and justice.

Therefore, the use of faith can lead to many different results. Sometimes the consequences of our faith are harmful, sometimes frivolous, and often helpful. Clearly, faith comes in many different qualities and it can produce starkly different effects. Therefore, the definition of faith depends on the context in which it is used and who is using faith.

What about spiritual uses of faith?

Religious organizations tend to assume they have an exclusive patent on faith and only allow the rest of us to use it occasionally. The truth is, faith is a generic part of the makeup of every person. Faith is part of the original factory equipment that is provided for every mature personality, much like our capacity for wisdom, courage, or joy.

The religious definition of faith can be briefly defined as:

1. The way to God, i.e., the means by which to attune ourself to God.

2. The measure of our belief in divinity and divine possibilities, i.e., the intensity of our faith is measured by the amount of loyal attention we give to divine direction and principles.

3. The spiritual lifestyle, i.e., the way of faith is to conduct ourself so that we have a continual reverence for the fact of the divine Presence in all people and behind all events—guiding us, supporting our worthwhile activities, and thwarting our base impulses.

The more *esoteric definitions of faith* are based on the understanding that there is a divine essence or presence about everything—no matter how imperfectly manifest it may be at the moment. In this sense, when we use faith as a noun, it is an aspect of devotional love. That is, faith is the ability to focus our devotion on the spiritual qualities or purposes (actual and potential) in any thing, person, situation, or concept.

When we use faith as a verb, however, the activity of faith becomes a way of living a life based on goodwill and hope of constructive possibilities. In other words, our thinking is proactive and mindful of our divine possibilities, our expectations are optimistic, our attitudes are nurturing, and our intentions are constructive. The esoteric use of faith is, therefore, the act of respecting and yearning for the potential for greatness and nobility in anything. While this can be formalized in ritual or words, it has no impact unless is it expressed as reverence for the divine possibilities in who we are and what we do.

Why is faith so powerful and important to us?
Faith, whether it is faith in good or bad potential, is important because faith *connects* us to things and *magnifies* our attitude and expectations about them.

Faith is, therefore, not a simple, innocent attitude we turn on and off at whim. Faith has the potential to commit our attention and involvement to whatever we believe is significant. This is why faith can be a power to attract and nurture the best—or the worst—in our self and our world.

Obviously, we can direct our faith to believe in the power of our problems and illnesses to destroy us. When we do, we magnetically attract and attune ourself to memories and expectations of fear, resentment, and despair. Even worse, we will increase their intensity by the very power of our belief. We can even attune ourself to antagonistic aspects of people and forces outside our personality. The net effect of these activities is to energize and sustain a dark mood in us. This can only lead to sabotaging our expression of strengths and promoting our defeat.

Fortunately, the reverse is just as true and possible. When we keep faith in the value and power of our talents, good efforts, and our opportunities, we are supporting our highest good. This is because we are magnetically joining ourself to our virtues and talents, sustaining our confidence, and focusing our attention on doing all the appropriate things that will support our success. Our faith then becomes an ally to strengthen the best in and for us.

Therefore, faith is a vital element of the mature personality, the successful lifestyle, and a productive relationship with anything, including our divine possibilities. Faith is what bonds us to our hopes and aspirations. Faith attracts good experiences to us and magnifies good qualities in us. Faith sustains right thinking and behavior while it neutralizes doubt and uncertainty. Faith is a major antidote to self-sabotage, cynicism, and despair. It is vital to the healing process.

Unless we understand and discipline our faith in constructive channels, it may easily undermine our well-being. Faith in negative forces and possibilities can readily bond us to misery and sickness. It will magnify our fears, faults, and failures while disabling our problem solving ability and dignity. Far too many people have more faith in their faults than their strengths, more faith in their failures than their achievements. In fact, faith is far more evident in most people by its connection to negative situations and its wrong use than in its constructive use.

Faith has a powerful potential for affecting or influencing a wide variety of our activities—work, health, and relationships to opportunities, people, challenges, and divine possibilities. The intelligent use of faith is indispensable to our success. Because of this, it is vital that we learn all we can about the constructive uses of faith and to recognize the presence of faith fatigue in us.

In the pressures of a busy life full of multiple responsibilities and some hardships, it is very easy to develop enduring disappointment, doubt, cynicism, and apathy. These are the signs that a major degree of faith fatigue has developed in us; we will need to reverse these tendencies as quickly as possible. In the next chapter, a complete portrait of the phenomena of faith fatigue will be presented.

Points to Ponder

1. How have you been using faith lately? Do you have more faith in the power of your problems and enemies than in your ability to manage them?

2. How often do you brood on a personal problem and discover that your bad mood or frustration seems to increase and spill over into other areas of your life and activities?

3. Have you ever noticed that your fear, sadness, and resentment *attracts* bad experiences to you rather quickly? Do you realize fully that devotion and gratitude will invoke and bond you to good experiences just as easily?

4. Is the quality of your faith in your good traits, abilities, and your higher self warm and frequent—or tepid and rare? Is this something you need to change?

chapter 2

What is Faith Fatigue?

Our beliefs color every relationship we have and the entire flow of our life. We have beliefs about the usefulness and value of every significant person, event, or situation in our life. We also have beliefs about what we expect to be doing. The quality of our faith in these things, therefore, has the power to control much about who we are, what we do, and how we respond to what happens to us.

As children, most of us begin life with a full charge of enthusiasm and eagerness to explore our personal world. While growing up, we hear a lot of voices telling us to stop doing something or warning us to stay away from specific areas, yet our strong charge of self-confidence, high energy, and natural resilience keeps us active and involved in all areas of life.

As we grow older and take on many new challenges, duties, and relationships, our opportunity to be challenged and fail increases. So also, as our range of experience and contacts increases, we are more likely to encounter criticism, resistance, and our own mistakes. The net result is that we have a growing burden of negative experiences and feelings to manage. Unless we learn to cope effectively with this challenge, we can suffer a major loss of our youthful enthusiasm and faith in the value of who we are, what we do, and what our future holds for us. Our faith is vulnerable to being strained, then exhausted, and finally wounded. Gradually, the phenomena of faith fatigue can overcome us.

The development of small measures of faith fatigue seems natural and logical at first. After all, the plain truth is that we get tired of disappointment, rejection, and frustration. We eventually give up trying to be better or attain something when we keep failing at our attempts. We get burned out from struggling and not achieving much. We feel drained when we are productive but fail to get either recognition or appreciation for our efforts.

Eventually, we can—in a few areas of our life—suffer from major degrees of exhaustion of our faith. We grow weary of the monotonous struggle of fighting off the petty behaviors of others and the apparent absurd obligations in our life. We get exhausted by the criticism or jealousy about us. We just become tired of being disappointed and discouraged in so many ways. Our life begins to seem empty and our struggle not worth our time and energy.

At this point, faith fatigue is the equivalent of an advanced stage of cancer—except this is a cancer in our personality and lifestyle. More specifically, it is a cancer that progressively destroys our confidence, self-esteem, and respect for anything. Life gradually become joyless and then a burden. The end stage is not just exhaustion, but a deep despair that excludes virtually all hope

This is how faith fatigue sets in and gradually diminishes the quality of our life.

Early Signs of Faith Fatigue

While the late stage of faith fatigue is easy to recognize, the early phase is far more subtle. Because faith fatigue—like most bad things—is very difficult to reverse once it reaches the late stage, it is important to recognize the early and faint signs of it. If we begin then to take steps to reverse our decline into strong doubt and despair, we will probably be successful.

In the early signs of faith fatigue, we may well believe we are dealing with something desirable, perhaps even mature and intelligent. We tell ourself that it is sensible to be extra cautious about new ideas, people, and opportunities. We assume that moderating our former enthusiasm is appropriate as we become more experienced and sophisticated in our knowledge. We presume that uncertainty about important decisions is a sign of wisdom and awareness of the complexity of life.

In fact, every step on our path toward faith fatigue can be rationalized. Every move toward hesitation and suspicion can seem natural and appropriate! What we fail to recognize is that it is never just our attitude that changes. We also begin to change our perspective, relationships, expectations, and involvement in the events of life.

When we are doubtful, our view of life narrows, and we begin to filter out too many potentials and opportunities because we consider them insignificant. We begin to disconnect from them or diminish their worth while magnifying the risk of failure.

When we are skeptical, our relationships are downgraded. Our confidence in our own strengths and abilities is weakened. Our trust in other people and groups is diminished. Our conviction that higher powers are favorable to our needs and struggles becomes less vigorous.

When faith fatigue begins, we also start to

lower our expectations. We expect less from our efforts and situations. We expect less recognition, approval, and compensation. Even worse, we begin to expect less joy and fulfillment from events and experiences that used to delight us.

As we believe in less, we expect less, and we do less. What may begin as a small disappointment can lead to a cascade of psychological events that ends in diminished achievement. Here the whole cycle of disappointment begins once again, but with renewed force and evidence that our life truly diminished in quality, meaning, and enjoyment.

The danger is that we tend to see only the external events and people who seem to have made life difficult for us. Too often, we ignore the fact that our burned-out faith has been the linchpin of the whole cycle.

The good news is that we can do many things to change ourself and prevent this descent into chronic dissatisfaction.

Why Are We Vulnerable to Faith Fatigue?
Recognizing the impending danger of faith fatigue is only part of what we must know to halt and reverse faith fatigue. We also need to understand how we enable the development of faith fatigue by what we do or fail to do.

Faith fatigue sets in so gradually and is so easily justified that many fail to notice its presence until it is well advanced in their attitudes and behavior. It is important that we learn to recognize the symptoms of faith fatigue and correct the process quickly. Unless we are vigilant, our doubt can turn into distrust and then paranoia. Caution will change into fear and then dread. Wariness will evolve into resentment and then alienation.

These attitudes do not emerge overnight, nor do they occur in isolation from our temperament or style of thinking and managing our life experience. In general, as we experience more personal challenges (real or perceived) to our authority, competence, appearance, activities, and beliefs, we accumulate wounds to our self-esteem and confidence. These are the challenges that can lead to faith fatigue unless we understand how to cope with these issues and events more effectively.

To accomplish this, we need more than clever strategies to cope with difficulty. We need to understand what must be fixed in ourselves and our habits.

The intelligent person soon recognizes that what irritates one person may well be tolerated by someone else. Where one person feels insulted, another easily ignores or accepts the same situation. And where one person is often overwhelmed by fear, another might be paralyzed by grief, and a third might react with overt rage.

Clearly, there are huge differences in the temperament of people and the kinds of situations that will bother them. Even more important is the fact that our habitual way of coping with severe stress will vary. This is where we need to identify our major vulnerabilities to being overwhelmed—the constant provocation for our faith fatigue.

Emotional people tend to respond to stressful events with fear, sadness, anger, or guilt. They cope by being obsessed with trying to avoid, rescue, defend, fix, and heal whatever seems wrong or broken—until they are worn out and then burnt out.

Mental people tend to have quite fixed ideas about what is right or wrong, when things are good enough or not, and when they and others have done enough. Their standards are often too high and their methods too rigid. They cope with severe distress with great frustration and an ever greater effort to figure out a way to fix things, until they impale themselves on their failure. Thereafter, they assume the mark of defeat and carry their scar as guilt and inferiority.

Strong-willed people expect to accomplish much and to do it their way. They cope by being intense, persistent, and unyielding. In times of stress, they become more intense, persistent, and angry. This stubbornness can easily lead to arrogance if successful or large accumulations of hostility and cynicism if unsuccessful. The late stages of both lead to deep disappointment.

To the degree people fail to modify or restrain the rough aspects of their personalities, they may develop ineffective coping styles that interfere with what is best for them. This failure leaves most people vulnerable to faith fatigue.

Anxious and depressed people tend to give up too soon and then protect themselves by avoiding risks, challenges, and opportunities. Doubt in their abilities and competence is their major vulnerability to faith fatigue.

Angry people distrust people and opportunities. Their uncooperative and rebellious attitudes (often totally unrecognized by them) provoke opposition and alienation in others. They then seek to protect themselves from further rejection and attack by being more cynical and isolated. Hostility and alienation from everything become their major vulnerabilities to faith fatigue.

Obsessive and perfectionistic people try to accomplish too much, too fast, and too soon. Their rigid demands on themselves and others exhausts everyone. They seek to protect themselves by working harder at less and less, and still they berate themselves about every shortcoming. Unrealistic expectations are the key vulnerabilities to faith fatigue.

As we develop greater understanding of ourself, we gain insight into the qualities we need to change to heal our faith fatigue. If we can discover and change the beliefs and habits in us that keep recreating faith fatigue, we will have taken a huge step on our path of recovery. Until we diagnose our special pattern of self-sabotage, we will be less able to do the things that build and sustain faith in ourselves and all good things. This is because good ideas and techniques will simply fall through our blind spots and become swallowed up by our distrust, fear, cynicism, arrogance, and despair.

Faith fatigue is a figurative cancer of our confidence, hope, and ability to assert ourself. Because these three elements are the underpinnings of all worthwhile endeavor, we cannot afford of neglect the role of intelligent and constructive faith in our life.

Because we are complex people—and life

experiences are even more complex—we do not have the luxury of one single technique which will work for all people. Just as there is no one size of shoes that fits all, there is also no single solution for faith fatigue that will work for all.

However, there are some *principles and rules* for the prevention and treatment of faith fatigue that are constant for all of us. These will be presented in the second and third sections of this book. These parts also give the details for how to repair faith fatigue when we doubt and despair about ourself, our situation, our past, and our divine opportunities.

Before we can be effective in treating faith fatigue, however, we need to know more about what makes us so uniquely susceptible to faith fatigue. This depends on our temperament and our usual coping style.

Points to Ponder

1. What is your usual method for coping with a stressful circumstance? Do you mainly complain, avoid situations and people, sulk in silence, or just retreat into self-pity? Is this the best you can do?

2. How often have you jeopardized yourself more than you have saved yourself by being withdrawn and passive or angry and demanding?

3. Do you recognize that you have more control over your emotional reactions and frustration than you have over the situations that triggered them? Is there a message in this fact for you?

4. Are you devoting more time to defending and expressing your anger, anxiety, or disappointment than you are trying to overcome them?

chapter 3

How Faith Works

While some people assume that having great faith is a worthy goal, we need to consider faith as a *means* to a worthy goal, rather than an objective by itself. Faith is a psychological and spiritual tool for working with the forces and qualities of life, including our own thoughts and feelings. Any tool, whether a literal tool like a hammer or a figurative tool like logic, has both proper and improper uses. The more we comprehend the inner mechanism of how effective faith operates, the more knowledge we will have to repair faith fatigue in ourself.

The Basic Activity of Faith

The primary function of the tool of faith is to attract and increase the force of what we believe is important or interesting. The attraction process can be directed towards any thing, person, situation, or idea. We can be delighted, frightened, or disgusted by what we perceive. We will therefore either attract ourself toward these forces and situations—or attract them to us. At the same time, we will increase the love, hate, fear, or grief we feel.

In other words, faith in the threat of some danger will increase our anxiety and draw us toward that threatening possibility or its equivalent. Faith in the support of our friends will increase our respect and appreciation for them as well as our attachment to them. Faith in a great plan for improving our career or a relationship will energize our enthusiasm for activating it as well as keeping our attention focused on what we need to do.

Faith can attract and energize qualities for others as well as ourself. Our faith in the ability of friends to cope with hardship will help energize their endurance and self-control. Faith in the ideals of good educational standards and practices can support excellence in education while motivating people to contribute more to the educational process.

Unfortunately, the process of attracting and increasing specific qualities and activities also works against us. Our faith that our illness will be fatal will direct fear to the body part that is sick (not a healing event) and increase our frustration. Our faith in the incompetence of an employee will increase his or her tendency to behave that way.

Obviously, the use of faith can help or harm us by nurturing good as well as bad potential anywhere. Faith can align us to our highest good, including our divine possibilities, just as easily as it can connect us to the worst in us and the situations around us. Since faith is easy to use, we need to learn all we can about the intelligent exercise of faith to promote our success and well-being and support health of our body and personality.

Varieties of Faith

Faith can vary much in quality and intensity. It is wrong to assume that faith is applied only to positive conditions and possibilities. For instance, our fear of disaster is merely faith in the possibility of a catastrophe. Grief is simply our faith in the fact that we have suffered greatly because of what we have lost or never had. Resentment is always accompanied by faith in the fact that we have been severely harmed—perhaps irreparably. Doubt represents our faith in the lack of value or genuineness of something. The full power of faith to attract and magnify our feelings about these matters can be used just as effectively for negative issues as for positive ones.

As there are differing qualities of faith, there are also many varying degrees of intensity and endurance in faith. Just as planes move faster than cars and cars move faster than bicycles, it should be obvious that faith also does not come in one "speed" or strength.

While any description of the different strengths of faith can be quite arbitrary, it is possible to measure the impact our faith has on our awareness, concern, and involvement.

The lightest, least powerful level of faith is when it only makes us aware of ideas, situations, and possibilities. Many people, for instance, have a very tepid belief in good ideas and possibilities. They may be intrigued by facts and certain possibilities; they may believe in divine potential or their own potential for a better career. But then they stop at this level, and go no further.

These people love to collect good ideas and suggestions, but then fail to take it to the next step of *using* good ideas and possibilities.

The medium level of power for faith is where we are concerned as well as informed about possibilities and ideas. In other words, we add enthusiasm to our awareness that we can be more successful in life if we do certain things. Or we add feelings of regret and remorse to our awareness that we have made huge mistakes.

The degree and quality of our concern can vary tremendously, but at least our concern pushes us out of the sterile realm of merely being aware of certain prospects. Now we not only notice something, we see the figurative red or green light flashing at us.

The most powerful stage of faith is when we add our involvement to our awareness and concern. When we are sufficiently aroused by what we notice, we will launch into action to protect, defend, or otherwise engage ourself in taking appropriate action. This is the stage when our faith comes alive as a powerful motivating factor that finally leads to significant change.

Knowing about these stages of intensity of our faith is significant in our effort to understand and reverse faith fatigue. One of the early stages of our decline into faith fatigue occurs when our faith in important matters is reduced to mere acknowledgement of ideas or possibilities. We no longer are very concerned about good or bad events or potential because we have retreated into apathy. We become indifferent about continuing irritations and no longer try to change things. We get tired of trying to cope with constant unfairness and interference and simply retreat into emotional numbness. We are neither committed nor concerned, because we are just trying to survive by—avoiding any response at all to whatever annoys us.

The foundation for this retreat into indifference is laid when we conclude that our situation is hopeless and we are helpless to change anything. Therefore, we just endure stoically. In our pessimism, we eliminate any attention to what we can do to change ourself when we cannot change our situation or our past. This stage goes beyond faith fatigue—it is the death of faith.

The Four Components of Effective Faith

Faith is not monolithic. There are four major parts to effective faith. When one or more of the parts is missing, we may only be wishing or fantasizing—not exercising genuine faith.

A common mistake many people make about faith is to assume it is primarily an attitude. They believe in certain possibilities and are enthusiastic or grateful about them. Or, they believe in danger and then anticipate it with fear and anger. This may seem to be the whole story of what faith is, but it is not. When we have an urgent need to repair faith fatigue, we must know the rest of the story about the mechanism of faith.

The quality of our focus of attention is only the first component in effective faith. There are three additional components that make our faith come alive as a powerful force. The second is *the expected result* that summons our interest and evokes a strong feeling. The third is *the source of power* or authority that has the capacity to exert a strong influence on our self or our situation. The fourth is *the actions we need to perform* to promote the result we want to achieve or avoid.

The source of power can be agents such as God, the government, a person, an enemy, nature, demons, an illness in our body, our proven strengths, or a chronic tendency to be anxious and uncertain.

The goal or the result we anticipate or want to avoid might be our health or sickness, our success or failure in a relationship, the growth or decline of our career, or our cheerfulness and serenity.

The activities we need to perform could be becoming more patient and tolerant, acting more assertively and persistently, intervening as a peacemaker instead of waiting for others to make all the concessions, learning to be a better listener or more cooperative, or changing our lifestyle.

When we add to all of these our attitude of conviction, trust, doubt, fear, like, or dislike, we then engage the full mechanism of faith. Our attitude and quality of attention will then perform several operations for us. They will *connect us to and summon* the power of whatever we believe in (e.g., a blessing, potential, threat, illness, or offer of support). They will also *connect* this power to us and the result we are expecting (e.g., health, sickness, trouble, success, etc.). In addition, our attitude and quality of attention will *motivate* us to begin doing the things that will support our expected result.

If we want to reverse our faith fatigue and make our faith effective and efficient, we need to have a clear understanding of each of these four components to effective faith.

If we fail to give sufficient attention to the source of power that can come to our aid, and instead, just eagerly imagine what we want, *we are only wishing.* Our faith will be weak and flabby, because there is no significant attention or attunement to a source of power to create change. Likewise, if we are expecting magical benefits to come to us without our involvement or effort, *we are only fantasizing.*

In both wishing and fantasizing the bulk of the concern is focused on what we want or dread rather than on the powers that might make it possible or what we might need to do to make it happen.

One of the major temptations that arises

when we have to cope with pleasant or unpleasant possibilities is the easy seduction of substituting wishing for genuine faith. The urgency of what we need or want becomes so overwhelming that we focus all of our attention on it. By default, we neglect both the powerful resources we must activate and what we should do to obtain the results we seek.

For example, it is common in religion to arrogantly assume that God wants what we want and will automatically give it to us if we merely wish for it. Of course, all of this is supposed to happen without any significant effort or sacrifice on our part. It is as if God does it all for us, and there are no steps between asking God for help and receiving what we want. Yes, occasionally, this is true, and we get lucky. But most of the time, this is not how it works. We may need to sacrifice most of our tendencies to worry, gripe, sulk, and blame before we achieve the tranquility and cheerfulness we seek. We may need to get to work and give up the comfort of blaming others for the emptiness in our life.

We will not be effective in healing our faith fatigue unless we recognize the need to repair all of the essential components of effective faith—*not just our attitude.*

The Allies of Faith

Another common misunderstanding of faith is that it is just about our *beliefs*—and beliefs are all about our *emotions*. Faith should be more than a collection of strong feelings. When we need a faith that works effectively in times of hardship and persistent distress, we need something more than a strong desire. We need allies to augment the strength and stability of our attitude. Fortunately, we can find the allies we need in our own mind and will. But we need to understand how the mind and will support and strengthen our faith.

The allies of faith we can discover at the mental level include trust, positive expectation, conviction, hope, focus, understanding, self-control, and various thinking skills. These attributes support faith in several ways. Greater understanding, for instance, can help us recognize the circumstantial evidence (proof) of what we believe to be possible for us. This adds conviction to our positive beliefs. Our mental faculties are also useful in developing an action plan for achieving what we want. Establishing very clear ideas of what we can do to contribute to our success will help eliminate doubt and build confidence in our impending success.

Our mind can also recognize other sources of power that can assist us—including our divine possibilities. The more we become familiar with these sources and understand them, the more we will trust in them and expect their support. As a result, we will automatically become more aligned and attuned to them. As we find them helping us achieve our goals, we will add conviction to our belief.

The will can also be a powerful ally of faith. The attributes of will that can strengthen faith are dedication, commitment, determination, intention, and perseverance. Intelligently used, the will can help us interpret our larger purposes into specific intentions and priorities. As we clarify and revise our plans and priorities through this use of the will, we are able to infuse our activities with far more of our personal and spiritual energies. The will likewise helps us preserve the discipline we need in order to achieve success. The will is also helpful as we dedicate ourself to working with higher forces. The will strengthens the process of aligning with spiritual forces and invoking them to aid us in our efforts. It strengthens our faith by adding commitment to belief.

The act of summoning these elements to strengthen our faith also helps us dispel hindrances to our success. Strong hope and enthusiasm alone may be insufficient to clear away any resistance we may meet in striving for our goals. We may need to express a strong measure of determination and commitment to defeat our own hesitation and doubts, reluctance to sacrifice our comfort, laziness, and unrealistic fears.

If we are going to increase the effectiveness of our faith and overcome faith fatigue, then we need to harness the right use of our allies in the mind and the will.

The Fourth Dimensional Dynamics of Faith

Because effective faith links subtle dimensions of life with the tangible, it is very easy to assume the mechanics of faith are comparable to mundane machinery. Nothing could be more erroneous. Effective faith can connect us to and summon a huge variety of invisible and intangible forces. These forces range from pools of fear and despair in mass consciousness—which the confirmed pessimist taps frequently—to the benevolence and power of God to lift up our mood and awareness to experience new degrees of confidence and health.

We need to comprehend clearly that there are invisible but real inner dimensions to the phenomena of life, and our intelligent use of faith can invoke aspects and qualities from this inner dimension.

A simple illustration of the importance of

faith in this process can be found in the process of growing tulips from bulbs. We know that if we plant tulip bulbs in the fall—with a bit of luck—they will bloom in the spring. And we know that if we plant tulip bulbs, we will get tulips—not carrots, cosmos, or cabbage. In some mysterious fashion, there seems to be an innate design or blueprint for making tulips hidden in these bulbs. This pattern or blueprint for "tulipness" is not a physical thing. It cannot be found under a microscope, because it is in a higher (i.e., nonphysical) dimension; yet, it has a tangible effect on the growing plant.

This blueprint is something like the recipe a cook might follow. However, as every good cook knows, recipes do not work by themselves; we need the right ingredients, right activity, and time to mix and cook the materials we have gathered.

Therefore, to the invisible blueprint in the tulip bulb (known to nature), we must add substance (soil and water), sunlight, the activity of the good gardener, and time for growth. If everything operates successfully, we will (whether we comprehend it or not) set in motion a fourth dimensional activity by which the inner, invisible blueprint of the tulip emerges as a mature flower.

The mechanism of faith does the same. *Faith*

is like sunlight to the growing tulip. Just as light draws out or invokes growth from the bulb, so also, our steadfast and positive faith can draw into manifestation whatever we seek. Yet, like the physical tulip, we also need the right substances or qualities plus intent, action, and the time to achieve the perfect result. The substance can be our contribution of knowledge and skill; the action can be our initiative, encouragement, and support.

Just as light stirs up growth in plants and draws them out of the soil by assisting the transformation of mud and water into mature plants, so also, we can use faith in our life. Faith can invoke and nurture our good potential and plans, and stir up good potential in our future. We can use faith to attract and energize our divine opportunities and summon our inner qualities into outer realization and expression.

How Faith Transforms and Heals Us

If we can understand that the right use of faith can summon higher potentials and qualities to us, then we can also recognize that this is the key to the process of transformation. More specifically, faith can support the transformation of our body and personality. This is the core activity in the process of healing and growth. For instance, faith in our strengths will support a healing transformation of our fear into calmness and confidence. Faith in our dignity and power to survive can heal and transform our anger into acceptance and forgiveness. Faith in new opportunities and achievements can heal and transform our apathy into hope and aspiration. Faith in what remains, what we can still do, and what lies before us can transform our grief about loss into new contentment and enthusiasm.

The Role of Faith in Mature Living

Faith is a major tool for manipulating forces of our consciousness to heal, transform, and enrich us—or demoralize and damage us. Fortunately, the right use of faith can support the best in us and also draw us closer to our Creator.

Faith has this potential because it can attract qualities and energies to us—including our divine possibilities. We can use these qualities to stabilize and strengthen our attention, intentions, and expectations. We can also use these qualities to transform our beliefs, attitudes, and habits. This, in turn, can assist us in transcending old (earthbound) ways of viewing ourself, our situation, our past, and our future.

In these ways, we can move closer to our

innate divine possibilities and potential about who we are and what we can be and do.

Points to Ponder

1. How intense is your faith in good possibilities? Is it enough to move you to action, or just to "be concerned?"

2. How often do you expect your faith to work by itself, i.e., without any significant action on your part to reach the goal you seek?

3. Do you understand how faith can transform fear into major distress as easily as it can transform forgiveness into compassion and a love of life?

4. How do you plan to use the transforming power of faith in your life?

chapter 4

How Faith Can Work Against Us

We often use our faith to undermine our best interests—generally, out of ignorance or misunderstanding. In some cases, using faith against ourself is a bad habit that we have had so long that we consider it normal—"normal" in the sense of being a constant complainer or being stuck in a persistent mood of self-pity and anxiety.

This is the reckless use of faith—to invoke and energize unhealthy qualities with chronic fear and worry, repeated feelings of remorse and regret, or recurring resentment.

Eventually, the negative use of faith can become as easy as breathing, especially if we allow our frustration and apathy to blind us to mature alternatives. When we reach this stage, it is possible to go through life using the tool of faith to harm ourself far more often than we use it in healthy ways. This is a common way good people slide into ever more frequent feelings of disappointment, regret, resentment, and hopelessness. Much of our faith fatigue begins this way and continues the rest of our life—until, that is, we become aware of what we are doing and begin to reform our understanding and habits.

Remember, faith is a tool for directing our attention, concern, and activities. Because there is much variation in our life experiences, there is also much disparity in the quantity and quality of our hopes, regrets, resentments, fears, and expectations. In other words, there can be great variation in what we believe and expect about people, events, and our potential—past, present, or future.

While this fact is neither new nor startling, its *significance* is worthy of scrutiny. Every time we focus our concern about any significant issue, we are also exercising our faith. In other words, our delight or dread about some future event represents the quality of our faith about it. When we regret or celebrate some past event, we are extending our faith to it. When we are contented or frustrated about some current event, we are again exercising our faith. All of these expressions are demonstrations of our usual quality of faith.

It is vital to grasp that we cannot merely

study the *theoretical* use of faith. We must also understand the *mundane* and *actual* uses of faith and their subtle potential to harm as well as help us. Recall that faith works by summoning and energizing the qualities (love, anger, fear, doubt, etc.) that are connected to the object of our concern. Therefore, our frequent negative use of faith may be sabotaging our highest good and diverting us from most of our resources for guidance, strength, talents, and ability to act creatively.

The Major Disorders of Faith

There are many ways to classify the misuses of faith. One approach is to group them around major negative attitudes:

1. Doubt and its aspects of cynicism, skepticism, and hesitation.

2. Fear and its aspects of anxiety, phobia, suspicion, and paranoia.

3. Resentment and its aspects of sarcasm, contempt, and alienation.

4. Sadness and its aspects of pessimism, hopelessness, and regret.

5. Guilt and its aspects of contrition and feeling unworthy and undeserving.

It is unfortunate that these attitudes are often rationalized as acceptable or even constructive (with their "right use" of course). This is because there are always people who would rather invent an excuse to avoid acting maturely than to be mature. These people enjoy creating new ways to redefine health and maturity to include the clever use of these negative traits. Many people slide into faith fatigue because they continually excuse their use of doubt, anger, fear, or sadness.

In truth, these attitudes are comparable to dirt and insects. They may well have a place in the world, *but not in our mental household.*

It is therefore far more effective to discuss the harmful uses of faith in a different context, by identifying the misuses of faith that lead to faith fatigue as follows:

1. We have too much faith.
2. Our faith is in inferior powers and ideas.
3. Our faith is too abstract and vague.
4. Our faith is concentrated on ourself.

By approaching faith fatigue in this way, we bypass the common willingness to rationalize negative attitudes and habits.

When We Have Too Much Faith

It is possible to be too confident as well as too humble. Or we can be far too enthusiastic as well as too discouraged. Any extreme or excess can lead to a reversal of fortunes brought about by our lack of moderation and balance.

People rarely complain about being too confident, optimistic, contented, or grateful. However, after their excessive confidence and enthusiasm has led to neglecting important duties and approaching problems, they can experience a major loss of faith in their abilities and activities. In some cases, faith fatigue develops suddenly and dramatically and goes on to deep despair and apathy. Most of the time, the collapse is gradual, but the fatigue of faith can become significant and often permanent.

Too much faith is more commonly seen in its negative usage. Most cases of too much faith involve the major slayers of good mental health and enlightened living: fear, doubt, anger, sadness, and guilt. That is, we have so much faith in whatever threatens us, thereby stimulating our fear, that we become paralyzed by it. Or we have so much faith that we will fail, thus feeding our doubt, that we quit at the first opposition and do not try again. Or we have so much faith that we have or are about to be insulted and abused by something, thus making us angry, that we become mired in blame and the desire for vengeance. Or we have so much faith that we are weak and incompetent, making us sad, that we give up and allow things to go unchallenged and unopposed. Or we have so much faith in the devastating consequences of our mistakes and inadequacies, thereby stimulating guilt, that we barely survive in humble underachievement.

Persistent negative faith—fear, doubt, anger, sadness, and guilt—is obviously not a state of faith fatigue. But it does lead to the excesses that produce exhaustion at the psychological level. That is, we end up in a weakened state where our ability to cultivate faith in anything is poor. The excesses of fear can exhaust us as surely as excesses of confidence. The same can be claimed for excesses of doubt, anger, sadness and guilt.

The less commonly discussed type of excessive faith occurs when we believe too enthusiastically and uncritically. That is, we trust and accept too much about a person, idea, practice, or authority. In other cases, we can believe too much in the value of a group—governmental, religious, or other.

When we become the *true believer*, we can fall victim to our own excess. The characteristics of true believers are:

1. They are intoxicated with their preferred beliefs—a state of virtual idolatry that does not tolerate opposing ideas, opinions, or practices.

2. They ignore facts and evidence that they are wrong.

3. There is a strong base of irrationality

and intellectual dishonesty (usually denied by them) that is essential to maintain their beliefs and practices.

Because they idolize what or whom they believe is correct, they filter out any criticism, facts, or results that invalidate their assumptions. They employ a large assortment of tricks to reject the significance of any challenging facts or evidence. They use remarks such as:

"It doesn't count."

"So what!"

"That's just your opinion."

"Nobody really knows for sure"...(so I will just keep believing what I want).

"Well, I am not aware of the ideas you are reporting"...(and don't want to be)!

These people have become intellectually dishonest. The truth does not matter any more to them because they assume they already have every part of it. Evidence that they have been wrong, fail to practice what they tell others to do, or fail to get the results they claim they seek is unimportant to them. This is because true believers base their confidence and certainty on their "wonderful intentions" and "brilliant theories." Any minor lack of achievement is merely a sign that they need to apply their efforts for a longer period or that the world is not cooperating. The possibility that they are profoundly misguided and mistaken is never even considered.

Blinded by such excessive faith, many people continue to follow inferior theories and practices that have a long track record of producing failure or harm. And worse, they continue to follow groups and support organizations that fail to provide the benefits they seek to produce. Thus we see those who claim to work for racial harmony and justice making obvious racist statements and promoting divisiveness. We hear from those who claim to work for gender equality and respect making obvious sexists statements about the opposing side. And we note the many politicians who claim they can cure everything by spending more money on it—even when there is constant evidence that their schemes are ineffective and wasteful.

The core problem of the true believer is that the emotions have overwhelmed the intellect and logic. Once they have established strong emotional preferences for what they want, they use the intellect only to rationalize what they want to believe.

Faith in Inferior Powers and Ideas

The experienced pessimist, the chronically anxious individual, and the perpetually indignant person who collects grievances all direct their faith to inferior powers and qualities. This occurs because their morbid attention and feelings are enthralled by the power of their illness, the threat to their marriage, the loss of business and income, their rejection by friends or family, or the dishonesty of others.

The eventual result of this enchantment is faith fatigue. Their great frustration about what is wrong or undesirable consumes the vast bulk of their resources to believe in anything. And even worse, their gloom, anxiety, and resentment metastasizes, like a cancer, to every major belief and relationship they have.

In these cases, faith fatigue will continue to build as they persist in distorting how they view life and evaluate their experiences. The two most common distortions are the habit of tunnel vision and the habit of giving excessive attention to what is undesirable.

Tunnel vision means that we tend to see issues or problems separate from the larger picture or context in which they happen. This implies that we are viewing a mistake or other disaster separate from its origins as well as the resources that can rescue and repair the damage. If we isolate our view of an unpleasant situation from what has happened before, we can easily miss the beginnings of current issues and events. If we have been ignoring ominous hints and trends that something bad is developing, then we have no right to act surprised and indignant when it occurs.

The worst aspect of tunnel vision is that it separates our issues and problems from the resources that we have to repair or modify them. When we are immersed in pain and suffering, we tend to exclude our capacity for hope, courage, and respect for what we still have and can do to help ourselves. Fear, anger, and sadness constrict our awareness so that our basic strengths and talents seem few, remote, or unavailable.

Finally, tunnel vision also excludes the benefit of a more long-term view of matters. A more detached perspective might, for instance, inform us that our issue or problem is actually a minor but hardly unexpected phase of a cycle which will soon become more favorable. Or better, the long range view might help us grasp that our issue is simply a part of our learning curve—a speed bump on the road of life that leads, inevitably, to greater growth and success.

The other distortion that induces eventual faith fatigue is the tendency to maintain a habitual imbalance of priorities and our focus of attention. The common way this manifests is to give more attention and significance to what is wrong and unpleasant than to what is good. It is not that we cannot recognize the difference between the two. It is just that we habitually tend to assume that when things are okay, this is the way they are supposed to be. No further attention is necessary. When things are bad, they become terribly important to us. Therefore, they command a huge amount of attention.

Unfortunately, the attention we usually give them is to complain, blame, or sulk. Instead of immediately assessing issues and seeking solutions and answers, we get stuck in our negative reactions and stay there indefinitely.

The danger of this situation is two-fold. First is that we summon and energize a large amount of anger, fear, or sadness. The second is that our distress tends to compel us to escape our distress more often than to solve our problem. This choice sends us down the path of searching for simplistic, quick solutions that do not address the underlying issues and long term trends.

Genuine solutions and cures are ignored.

When Our Faith is Too Abstract

It is possible for our faith to be focused on ideas and possibilities that are too vague and theoretical. Examples can be found in the fuzzy thinking idealist, the mystic lost in otherworldly generalities, and the philosopher who is consumed by grandiose theories and solutions. The objects of their faith are vague, abstract, and hypothetical. Many of these types of people are found in the realm of academia where they can indulge in the philosophy of government, religion, art, education, good, and evil.

There is nothing inherently wrong in speculating about the inner side of life or the archetypal principles behind religion, government, art, or human behavior. It is just that we must eventually come to terms with the concrete and objective issues of the world we live in. However much we prepare ourself with general theories and good possibilities, we need real, not theoretical, solutions to practical problems and issues. We need concrete plans and details about what to do, not just abstract beliefs and hopes. Great achievements may begin with noble theories and ideas, but they end with most of the attention and effort being applied to specific strategies and activities essential to achieving these goals.

Many will fail to see this trend or their lack of pragmatism. They will claim that they are working very diligently on their health, career, or relationships. The fact that they do not have any solid results to demonstrate rarely bothers them. These people make the mistake of assuming that their belief, theories and good intentions are so wonderful, that just their belief in them is all they need to do. And if they do anything at all, then only good results can come from any of their efforts.

In other words, their great ideas and intentions justify everything they do or fail to do. Because they lack a pragmatic perspective, they tend to assume that their theories and ideals need no proof. Certainly, the bad consequences of their intentions and theories are never seen as evidence that they are mistaken. They have become the true believer who has a self-created license to ignore results. They are "beyond" doubt.

Of course, they are also beyond reason, logic, accountability, and reality.

Their faith is now in illusions, delusions, and self-deceptions.

Faith fatigue is common when our faith becomes too abstract or is focused on very distant objectives because it often ends as well as begins in the intangible realms. As wonderful as it is to believe in the ideals of justice, charity, and goodwill, our belief is no substitute for the work needed to make a practical demonstration of the results we seek. Eventually, our failure to achieve these distant goals causes us to lose, first, our enthusiasm for them, then our interest, and finally, our attention.

Our faith fatigue is now complete.

When Our Faith is Too Personal and Selfish

When we are caught up in the habit of self-absorption, we are entering into a very small world. Continual narcissism tends to make us view life only in terms of what is good or bad for us. Outer events and other people seem to have little significance, except for their potential to help or harm us.

The small world of egomania is ruled by the the desire to avoid unpleasantness and the desire to feel good, i.e., safe, comfortable, adored, supported, and protected. The basis for judging everything is whatever feels good, flatters, or helps us to get what we want. The truth, when unpleasant to see or hear, is rejected. Evidence of our selfishness, lack of responsibility, and destructive behavior is ignored. Any criticism or threat to our self-esteem is considered as a personal insult. The need to feel good can trump any idea, fact, or logic we dislike.

If we are unable to cope with criticism, rejection, loss, or even the truth, we suffer from a profound weakness. This deficiency makes it progressively more exhausting to sustain faith in the value of who we are and what we are doing. We have to put more and more effort into blaming others for the fact that our life is far less than it should be. We wrap ourself in the identity of being a victim of the abuse or neglect of others and then respond by sulking. Thereafter, we will need to spend more energy in avoiding the truth and keeping up excuses. We will have to work harder to preserve old rationalizations and invent new ones to protect ourself from the fact that we are so far less successful and productive in key aspects of our life than we should be.

This introversion of attention and concern produces a focus of faith that concentrates on personal wants, desires, and frustrations. Most of this will attract and intensify our discouragement, resentment, and self-pity.

None of this contributes anything to our happiness, maturity, or health. All it does is create a slow decline towards emptiness and apathy. Instead of keeping faith in our opportunities, strengths, and talents, the focus of concern is on the good that is missing, lost, or never happened—and the bad that is present. Faith is still present, but is directed to our awareness of undesirable things and the threat of abandonment.

The crucial point at which faith fatigue will dominate our life is when we come to have a stronger belief in the continuity of our burdens and wounds than in our recovery. First we stop believing in the support of others. Then, we lose faith in our ability to cope. Later, we come to believe that there is nothing in our future except perpetual problems and frustrations. And finally, we believe in nothing much at all. Faith fatigue is then complete.

The Way Out of This Misunderstanding

The misuse of faith to increase our misery is unfortunately common. It happens every time we linger too long in resenting what we dislike, fearing threats, being discouraged about our lack of success, or otherwise feeling sorry for ourself. The fact that these responses are often rationalized as being normal and appropriate indicates how much we have to unlearn.

Every mature person—from time to time—has to confront genuine losses, illnesses, mistakes, and the harmful acts of others. Human nature, our own or that of others, is far from perfect. The same can be said for society. It takes little genius or creativity to spot the flaws in one another or society. But genius and much creativity does seem to be essential to find and implement the work necessary for constructive, proactive approaches to the common unpleasant issues of life.

There is absolutely no reason why we cannot establish better habits for coping with whatever discourages or defeats us. All it takes is the intelligence to mobilize the best of our skills and virtues, as well as the determination to invest them in our life.

Points to Ponder

1. How often do you ignore consistently poor results in what you do just because you cannot tolerate being wrong?

2. Do you have more faith in your tendency to fail or to succeed in key areas?

3. Do you tend to idolize your ideals without putting them to work in your life?

4. Are you more concerned about what others can do for you or what you can do for yourself?

chapter 5

The Basis of Healing Faith

The first rule for making effective change is to start where we are and use the resources we have. It is pointless to study esoteric theory and techniques if they are outside the range of our understanding and experience. Therefore, let us begin with the assumption that we have pinpointed areas in ourself and our self-expression that we would change if we could.

Let us proceed from this point in the full understanding that effective change will come about largely *by what we do about ourself*—not just our situation. Many people endure huge amounts of frustration and disappointment because they labor mainly to fix outer conditions or other people—or even society—*instead of themselves.* In other words, we must face the truth about ourself and do something about the areas of belief, attitudes, and intentions within us that need improvement.

The Two Major Rules of Learning

If we intend to make a serious effort to re-evaluate ourself and amend our beliefs and habits, we must accept the two major rules of learning. *First, we must be open to new ideas.* To be open to new ideas means that we will give them our full consideration—not that we automatically accept them. Too many people resist new ideas and techniques for the most fickle of reasons. They claim they do not like them because they involve too much work or sacrifice. Or the ideas seem to contradict what they prefer to believe. And by these whimsical criteria, they reject far too many new concepts and behaviors.

The second rule of learning is *we must be willing to admit that we have been wrong.* Egotism is often a major stumbling block to effective learning and change. When we make major changes in our beliefs and behaviors, this suggests that what we have been believing or doing was wrong. This in turn, implies that we have not been very wise or efficient—an unbearable admission for some. Such people neglect the fact that it can be even more embarrassing to continue with inferior beliefs and activities and all the consequences that they produce.

The healing of our faith fatigue needs to begin with our current beliefs and habits. These, we must assume, have been shaped primarily by our personal experiences. It is no great revelation to state that major events and situations in our life foster the development of specific beliefs and patterns of response to what happens to us. These beliefs and habits—for better or worse—are clustered around how we view our self, what happens to us, what we do, and our major relationships with key people, authorities, hardships, and opportunities, including our divine opportunities.

It is very common for the average person to be deeply affected by the power of old wounds, losses, and embarrassments. We are also heavily influenced by the power of illness, hostile groups, and our own limitations in managing them. Our talents and successes also have an impact on our beliefs and attitudes, but usually not as much as our own deficiencies. Finally, the strength of our relationship to divine possibilities can be a major factor in the quality of our beliefs, understanding, and faith.

Collectively, the beliefs we develop about all of the above have the power to create and recreate within us endless sadness or joy, fear or courage, anger or forgiveness, and guilt or fulfillment. This means that no matter how clever we become in manipulating our outer situation, we will be dragging our beliefs in doom, our fear of failure and abandonment, and our resentment of criticism into everything we do and achieve. Every bit of success we attain will be polluted by these beliefs and habits. Even worse, the potential consequences of our unreformed fears, doubts, resentments, and grief can intrude at any time to sabotage us—especially in times of stress, fatigue, and illness.

Until we recognize that this is how we create our own suffering and then make the right changes, we will make little progress in improving our lives. This is because our faith in the validity of our gloom, fear, doubt, anger, alienation, and inferiority will tend to be self-perpetuating. For instance, the hostile person will keep alienating people and avoiding opportunities to create harmony. The anxious person will continue to be defensive and complicate life by continual suspicion and fear of risks. And the pessimistic person will continue to miss opportunities as well as satisfaction in what little he or she achieves.

The most famous example of using the two major rules of learning is found in the story of the Prodigal Son. Only after he had endured profound suffering did he realize that he must consider a whole new perspective about life. This then led to his epiphany of comprehending how he had been profoundly wrong in his understanding and expectations. Immediately, he "rose up" in this new understanding and began his path of redemptive change.

Like the Prodigal Son, we need to accept the fact of our own faulty beliefs and choices as the root of most of our suffering. We must then rise up in our awareness and beliefs to accept a new view of our human and divine potential and destiny for greatness. As we do this, our response to life—past, present, and future—changes dramatically and for the better.

Points to Ponder

1. Are you always waiting for a "better" time and "better" conditions before you begin earnest work on self-improvement? Do you recognize that this is just a way of resisting change?

2. When you meet with difficulty, do you automatically assume that only the situation needs fixing, or do you also wonder if something about your beliefs and behavior might need adjustment?

3. How open to new ideas are you? Can you identify where you have caused yourself considerable distress by choices and reactions that sabotaged your highest good?

4. How difficult is it for you to admit you have been wrong? How often does this resistance get in the way of accepting the truth?

Part Two: HEALING THE FAITH KILLERS

chapter 6

Healing Doubt and Hesitation

If we were to try to discover why our car does not start, we would need to examine the engine compartment. Looking under the front seat or in the trunk would not likely provide any useful information. In the same way, we need to check out key areas of our beliefs and habits that can prevent our faith from starting to work for us in reliable and effective ways.

There are four types of beliefs and habits that become faith killers. We need to know all about them and how to manage them, because they are present everywhere and in everyone. Until we hunt them down and control them, faith fatigue will be a constant problem for us.

The four most notorious faith killers are:

1. Doubt and its evil twin, hesitation.
2. Ignorance.
3. Laziness.
4. Rationalization.

Signs of Doubt and Hesitation

Doubt and hesitation are the twin demons which often undermine faith and produce faith fatigue. Doubt weakens our faith in our talents, strengths, and choices. Hesitation diminishes our ability to act, to make decisions, and to express our talents. Both lead to missed opportunities, lukewarm involvement, and underachievement.

At the physical level, doubt manifests as hesitation in asserting ourself in times of challenge or resistance. We may be concerned about making mistakes or offending others. Or we may be uncertain that we can do what we hope to achieve, or simply be unsure about whether we have the time, authority, or skill to accomplish what we intend to do. In every instance, hesitation can act as a brake on our capacity to act in an appropriate and timely fashion. Frequent hesitation in us is a certain sign that we need to clarify our thinking and strengthen our motivation to act.

At the emotional level, doubt manifests as fear and feelings of misgivings about what we have done, are doing, or are planning to do. That is, we fear that our action or lack of action might offend others or embarrass ourself. In mild cases, we may only have to contend with anxiety as a constant companion in whatever we do and say. In severe cases, doubt can damage not just our confidence—it can restrict our self-expression to the point of extinction.

In other instances, doubt will be present, but unrecognized, in the form of emotional numbness. This occurs most often after long periods of fear and despair have exhausted us into near emotional emptiness. Emotions are not suppressed, they are just depleted. The certain evidence of emotional exhaustion is that wonderful news and events fail to elicit the appropriate excitement and enthusiasm in us. Numb emotions are a sign that our faith will also be very fatigued—if not on life support.

In all cases of emotional doubt, there is an urgent need to reevaluate our priorities. This will help us by isolating the truly important matters in our life so we can focus our limited energies on them.

At the mental level, doubt manifests as cynicism and skepticism. We are uncertain about the validity, accuracy, or authenticity of ideas, theories, plans, or evidence presented to us. Unreasonable degrees of skepticism usually are focused in the areas where we already have established strong beliefs and habits. These are the part of our thoughts and feelings that we have converted into dogma. This represents where we are clearly biased in favor of our own opinions and beliefs, and we do not appreciate anything that seems like an attack on them.

Skepticism also occurs when we suspect we are being manipulated, for whatever reason. Our mental antennae are alerted to the possibility that an offer or explanation sounds too slick, too good to be true, or too far outside the realm of our experience to be valid.

When skepticism begins to interfere with our ability to be open to new ideas and accept change, we need to challenge some of our assumptions. We may need to speculate that many aspects of the *truth* may also be outside the realm of our experience. In addition, we may need to wonder if we are too strongly invested in certain values, opinions, and sets of beliefs. Could we be prejudiced—not just opinionated?

At the spiritual level, doubt manifests as agnosticism. The concept of a Creator and benevolent Deity may be accepted, but we do not engage in traditions or beliefs. We may profess a tepid belief, but underneath, we do not expect much. We may be going through the usual motions of prayer and worship, giving lip service to dogma, but we expect little or nothing to change. Spiritual principles, ethics, and practices are notable mainly by their absence.

How Doubt and Hesitation Take Root

Many people rationalize their doubts because they presume it is sensible to be cautious and thoughtful about what they are doing and planning. But there is a practical limit for using doubt to prevent mistakes. Doubt quickly becomes the assassin to hope, assertiveness, and accomplishment.

There are several basic reasons why we might harbor excessive doubt and hesitation. The first is that we are fearful about new situations because we are still "in mourning" for past disasters and embarrassments. Something in us still reverberates to old wounds, losses, and mistakes. That is, the ghosts of old psychological wounds are still actively distorting our perceptions, interpretations, and choices.

These experiences are often accompanied by inhibiting or limiting beliefs *which are appropriate only to those old, unpleasant times.* For instance, a child may decide (appropriately) that he or she must never risk the disapproval of adult authority. In our adult years, however, this limiting belief can strangle our assertiveness more often than it saves us from condemnation and loss of love and privileges.

The second major reason why we harbor excessive doubt is that we are too intolerant of ambiguity. We demand clarity, certainty, and guarantees of correctness and safety before we proceed with a decision or commitment. There is nothing wrong with expecting clarity and full disclosure of available facts and possibilities. However, our ability to decide *when we have enough* information to make an interpretation or decision can be too demanding and neurotic. Perfection is rarely necessary or desirable. With certain notable exceptions, perfectionism limits us and decreases our productivity and fulfillment far more often than it improves our performance and efficiency.

The third reason why we are too doubtful and hesitant is our excessive and inappropriate fears. These can be quite ordinary fears such as fear of failure, rejection, loss, or embarrassing mistakes. When these fears become excessive and unrealistic, they can become a prison to our freedom and fulfillment.

The fourth major justification for embracing excessive doubt is the presumption that we do not have the knowledge, skill, or experience to succeed. But this is more of an excuse than a legitimate reason to miss a valid opportunity. Even if it were true, a legitimate response would be to push ourself to acquire the needed knowledge, skill, and experience—not give up.

Managing Excessive Doubt and Hesitation

Because unrealistic doubts are a constant companion of faith fatigue, we need to challenge our assumptions to determine if they are still valid. We may need large amounts of intellectual honesty and courage to be effective in this review.

When we challenge any of our beliefs or assumptions, we must be careful to avoid the popular psychobabble claim that our *perceptions* are what is real. This is the sort of nonsense that got us into trouble in the first place; we must strongly and persistently reject it. For instance, we might have some dark imaginings that everyone is secretly snickering at our clumsiness. Just because we imagine something *does not* make it true or valid. However, if we choose to act as if it were true, we may well create difficulties for ourself. This mischief is undone only as we challenge our beliefs and insist on imposing the truth.

We can begin contesting our limiting beliefs by determining if we would truly like to do more, achieve more, or become better at some activity or characteristic. This process begins by questioning whether our problem is a genuine limitation in skill or authority—or just our own inhibition. This will help us distinguish between realistic and unrealistic fears.

In addition, we need to check our memories for when we first decided that we could not do or be something. This helps us understand if we are basing our beliefs on old information, i.e., the ancient situations we used to endure and the limited skill and freedom that were present at that time. Too many fail to realize that our thinking and attitudes are stuck in a time warp when we were in a state of reduced circumstances, abilities, and opportunities. Yet, we are still acting as if all of those limitations and deprivations are still with us. When we take more time to dwell on how we and our circumstances have changed, we can release ourself from old limiting beliefs and give ourself permission to be more emancipated and assertive.

If our doubts have some validity—i.e., we assume we actually do lack strategic skills, knowledge, and experience—then we have two choices. First, we can adapt our activities to fit the strengths and skills we have and become as productive as possible. Or we can encourage ourself to expand our knowledge and otherwise acquire the experience that leads to greater skill and competence.

If we are forever fussing about the need for more information, more proof, and more guarantees before we can proceed, then we must acknowledge our habit of perfectionism and intolerance to ambiguity. The bad news is that these are difficult habits to change; the good news is that we can use cleverness and skill to overcome them.

The cure to perfectionism is to change the goal from absolute perfection to the pursuit of excellence. Excellence is defined as the best we can do under current circumstances. Excellence is usually achievable, and our good results tend to increase our self-confidence. Conversely, perfection is rarely achievable, and so it tends to cause us to feel discouraged and increase our sense of inadequacy.

The key to changing the habit of perfectionism is to review our criteria for deciding when we have enough. That is, when do we have enough information to make a decision, enough experience to trust ourself, enough time to complete a task, enough preparation to begin our tasks, or enough power and courage to finish a task. Usually, we can root out all kinds of absurd standards that have become the basis for unrealistic expectations and fears. Eventually, we must accept that ambiguity is an integral part of life. We can reduce it somewhat, but it is usually futile to try to eliminate it from our thoughts and activities.

In general, the cure for excessive doubts and

hesitation comes about as we challenge ourself to modify our expectations and activities and demand realistic changes. When we properly encourage ourself to do this, the solutions begin to become clear. The transformation is usually gradual and requires persistent attention. Some, however, will find that performing this review will bring about an epiphany that leads to significant breakthroughs in reviving their confidence and enthusiasm.

If we lack motivation to begin and continue this review and monitoring process, there are two steps we can take to overcome excessive doubt. First, we can dwell on the anticipation of receiving the extra benefits of achieving more because we have eliminated doubt and hesitation. Second, we can review the continued disappointment and suffering we will endure if we do not change. Both realizations can become powerful incentives for the successful management of our excessive doubts and fears.

If we think and act in this way, we will begin to make significant progress in reducing the presence of doubt and hesitation in our makeup and behavior.

Points to Ponder

1. Do you just accept all of your doubts and rationalizations for being so cautious, or are

you in the habit of questioning their validity?

2. Is some part of your beliefs stuck in the past where you still think and act as if you are as limited and wounded as you once were? Are you being fair to yourself?

3. Are you demanding too many proofs and guarantees for your safety and success before you decide to act?

4. Have you considered how much success and enjoyment you are missing when you doubt and hesitate too much? Is it time to change yet?

chapter 7

Healing Ignorance

The second major "killer" of intelligent faith is our lack of knowledge and skill. Wise people have told us for millennia that knowledge can add strength, clarity, and direction to our faith. Knowledge helps us understand *what to believe in* (sources of power, authority, principles), *what we are doing*, and *why any of this is important*. This kind of knowledge is a powerful weapon to defeat faith fatigue because it empowers us and focuses our resources precisely where we can be most effective.

While there are a myriad of things we need to know, the minimum of general knowledge we need to have to combat faith fatigue include:

1. The rules of pessimism and optimism.
2. The laws of attention and concentration.
3. The nature of health and maturity.
4. The basis of our human and divine potential.

5. What we need to stop doing and begin doing.

The Rules of Pessimism and Optimism

There are common sense observations about pessimism and optimism that seem to elude far too many intelligent people. These "rules" define the consequences of these attitudes.

The rules of pessimism suggest that we can *always* find some fault or inadequacy in everyone and anything and plenty of reasons to justify this judgment. And by doing so, we can always make a bad thing worse by concentrating on its bad features and ignoring its good qualities and potential. Millions of people demonstrate the power of these rules every day by their selective and gloomy focus of attention, and their enjoyment in finding something new to add to their list of grievances. Some do it to prove how superior they are in their standards and powers of observation. Others do it to distract attention from their own faults. And still others do it to boost their fragile self-esteem and to justify a brief moment of moral indignation. A few seem to do it just to create trouble.

Most of the time, complaining and fault finding is just a habit, and a stupid one at that. This is because these activities simply stir up and increase frustrations, animosities, divisions, and distress. It interferes with solving problems, effective communication, and the healing of minds, hearts, and bodies. The worst aspect of gloomy attitudes and fault finding is that it kills our faith in the worthy aspects and potential in our self, work, talents, opportunities, and relationship to higher powers.

This is not an intelligent thing for anyone to do. A bit of reflection and consideration about these habits should convince us that we need to monitor ourself for these tendencies and stop them permanently. Fortunately, we have the rules of optimism to help us.

These rules are the counterpart of the rules of pessimism. In other words, we can always find something *good* to praise about everyone and anything. This can be praise for both actual or potential value in what we perceive. Likewise, we can always improve matters with praise and gratitude. Praise and gratitude lubricate relations, improve communications, facilitate creative thought, and energize our vitality. Best of all, the habits of praise and gratitude liberate and strengthen our best qualities, stimulate our mature characteristics, augment our anticipation of productivity and add to our fulfillment in life. Mature optimism is the hallmark of successful people. It is a powerful tool for resurrecting our wounded faith and restoring it to full working condition.

Far too many are reluctant to express honest praise because they fear that others will interpret this as a sign that they are forgiving all past grievances and complaints. Secretly, many are reluctant to feel or give sincere praise for fear that they will lose their reputation of being "strong" and "unrelenting." Of course, they fail to understand that others interpret these traits, respectively, as being grumpy and stubborn.

The effective reversal of faith fatigue will depend on getting control of our tendencies to think, believe, interpret, and act in a pessimistic manner. If we have to strain to be more optimistic, it will be worth the effort, and we will quickly acquire the evidence of its value in our personal experience.

The Law of Attention and Concentration

Laws are as different from rules as the force of gravity is from the rules for vehicle traffic. One originates in Universal Powers and Order that are entirely independent of our human awareness, preference, or choice. The other is dependent on the design and consensus of many people. Rules can be debated or ignored, but Universal Laws have to be obeyed.

The Law of Attention states that our focus of thought, feeling, and intention will direct the energies of our ideas, emotions, and will. Therefore, if we concentrate on our pain and misery, we will direct the force of our beliefs toward our own suffering. The usual result is an increase in our distress.

Fortunately, we can also concentrate on the joy we anticipate in a weekend trip or the completion of some project. This activity will focus the energies of cheerfulness and enthusiasm in ourself as well as toward the experiences we are expecting.

We all have the power to concentrate and project the power of our thoughts and feelings. This requires no special talent at all. Anyone can fall from a chair—dead or alive—because the law of gravity ordains it. In a similar fashion, even morons can brood on fears about their next trip to a dentist, and easily stir up a bad mood and a headache as a consequence.

Agonizing about our inadequacies, failures, and losses will produce only a bad mood. This bad mood will depress our creativity and ability to act with effectiveness and efficiency. Brooding on what is wrong and what we cannot do and do not have will also depress our vitality, diminish our joy, and constrict our vision of what is still possible for us.

Most importantly of all, concentrating on our failures and faults will damage or kill our faith. If we are to be successful in reversing our fatigue of faith, we will need to adapt our habits and begin working with the Law of Attention as an ally. More specifically, we need to give more attention to the opportunities, strengths, and talents we have than to our problems, hardships, and weaknesses. This will boost our conviction that there are many worthy elements in us and what we do. As we make a habit of persisting in this style of focusing our attitudes and thought, we will build up a strong and constructive focus for our faith.

The Nature of Health and Maturity
A major mistake many people make about the nature of health and maturity is the assumption that they are defined largely by the absence of any symptoms or complaints. In other words, if we have a high energy, pain free body, we are healthy. And if we are calm, free of guilt, fear, and inhibitions, we must be mature and possess psychological health.

This might be true for a domesticated cat or dog or even a small child, but it falls far short of a sensible definition of health and maturity in an adult. Health is a whole lot more than just not being sick. And maturity is a whole lot more than being comfortable and able to express any emotion we want without guilt.

Many confuse what is *common* with what is normal and healthy. It is common for elderly people to become tired, arthritic, and limited in activity, but this does not mean it is healthy for them. Just because many people tend to be gloomy does not mean this is a mature response to life. So also, being angry after every insult or mistake is common, but this is neither mature nor healthy.

These issues have been confused in recent decades by those who like to pander to the confused and anxious by telling them to accept themselves the way they are. Self-acceptance is a virtue, but if we lower the standards merely to relieve a few feelings of guilt and grief, we are abandoning our aspirations and dignity for cheap comfort. A criminal can *feel* good by doing less and being less. But *being* good, i.e., being healthy and mature, is radically different. Feeling good is a minor consequence of being healthy—not a sign or criterion of health and maturity.

Health and maturity both depend on the cultivation and expression of virtues such as intelligence, integrity, tolerance, self-control, courage, endurance, patience, sensitivity to the needs of others, accountability, adaptability, love, joy, and a capacity for commitment and loyalty. A person who is occasionally anxious or discouraged has these virtues, they are still mature and healthy.

Health and maturity must include a developed mentality in which we have the capacity to *recognize* our strengths, blessings, opportunities, and duties. It also includes the ability to *respond* to these matters with as much intelligence, compassion, and courage as possible. If we can do these things to be productive and useful in the world, we are probably quite healthy and mature in mind, body, and spirit.

True health and maturity is all about our dynamic ability to be productive at mental, emotional, and physical levels. A few minor emotional symptoms and problems need not disqualify us as being healthy. We need to view health and maturity from the standards of how often we can invest joy in life and how much we can contribute to life and be fulfilled by who we are and what we do.

The practical significance of a more enlightened definition of health and maturity is that it broadens and elevates the standards we need to use to evaluate our self and our situation. We need not lose faith in ourself if we are able to manage our responsibilities and do good work in spite of our discouragement or self-doubts. We need not allow arthritis or other minor complaints to ruin our day if we understand our life and existence is far more than our bones and joints and how we feel. We need not allow our lack of understanding or experience make us feel inadequate if we are able to be useful in the world and attend to our responsibilities in spite of this.

How we perceive our health and evaluate our maturity can be a vital factor affecting the state of our faith. As we add to our understanding, we can eliminate much unnecessary discouragement. In these ways, greater knowledge helps us overcome faith fatigue.

Human and Divine Potential as a Resource

One of the great tragedies of life is that most people assume they are a product entirely of their earthly experiences and the life of their physical body. Even worse, they tend to assume that their failures, losses, and illnesses are far more significant than their successes and health. Consequently, good people often devote more time to being annoyed about what is wrong with their life than they spend in celebrating their achievements and blessings.

No where is this gloomy bias more poignant than in the areas of our human and divine potential. By default, we tend to assume that we have a huge potential for pain, suffering, failure, and defeat. Our potential for health and success, however, is limited.

Most of us are not ignorant of the positive side of our human potential and divinity. The problem is that we tend to consider it as a very remote possibility—more theoretical and speculative than actual. We do not, therefore, expect much help from it. If we expect little and believe in even less, we are only denying ourself access to many powerful resources that we need to heal and enrich our life.

Such profound ignorance is a major killer of faith.

The truth is that our higher potential is a blend of the best of both our human and divine natures. It is pointless to try to separate them at this level. As such, the combined force of these two aspects of our nature is a rich source of wisdom, love, joy, courage, patience, and self-control for us. And, contrary to many theologians, it is reasonable to expect to summon and activate these qualities in ourself.

Unfortunately, more people rely on ignorance and wishful thinking than practical wisdom in approaching these issues. The same can be said about the methods used to summon inner resources. Some people naïvely assume that higher powers will come only when God decides, and all we need to do is believe and wait. So, they just keep hoping and waiting to get lucky! Others believe that a few positive thoughts are all that will be necessary for making the connection.

Long experience indicates that our higher potential for anything—especially wisdom, courage, and love—*will come as we seek to act in these ways.* That is, we need to add to our own deep yearning for wisdom an active search for it. We need to long to be more confident and tranquil about the burdens we bear, and struggle to behave that way as often as possible. We must also strive to become more effective and creative in helping others.

These kinds of aspirations to be a better person and be more helpful are common ways that good people respond to their spiritual will. The net result is a very powerful invocation of the best of our human potential and everything in our divine potential. As we persist in our determination to be and do better things, we activate these potentials in who we are and what we do.

This is the core principle of working with our higher potentials. It does much to renew our faith at all levels.

What To Stop Doing—and Begin Doing

The common myth about self-improvement is that we just need to engage in a bit more positive thinking and feeling, and then all will be better. The depressed person is told to be more cheerful. The anxious person is encouraged to be more confident and relaxed. The angry person is told to be more tolerant and calm. It all sounds logical and appropriate, but this is never more than half the story—and usually less.

If we want to improve ourself and our situation, what we need to stop doing is often just as important—or more so—than what we are supposed to begin doing. Angry people will probably improve fastest by making a major effort to restrain their tendencies to complain and condemn. Depressed people will benefit most from the effort to stop living in the past and feeling sorry for themselves. Anxious people will best recover if they stop fussing about trivial matters as if they were significant. Many ill people benefit more by giving up destructive lifestyle practices than any medication the patient might take.

Old habits usually do not quietly fade away. They stay alive and defend themselves—sometime quite vigorously. Despite this tendency, there are times when we need to recognize that we are still contributing to our own distress. Then we need to stop it. To do less would be stupid and dishonor our humanity.

Conscious ignorance and subconscious ignorance (often called denial) are powerful killers of our faith in all good things. But even worse, ignorance often kills far more than our faith. Ignorance and denial can kill or damage our health, peace of mind, and joy in living.

Only the truth can set us free of these limitations.

Points to Ponder

1. Do you lapse into pessimism too often? Do you have a plan to monitor these lapses and correct them?

2. Are you more concerned about the constructive things you can do or what is wrong in your life?

3. How do you usually regard your higher potentials for wisdom, courage, and love? If you occasionally think of them, do you expect much from them?

4. Have you fully considered both what you need to stop doing as well as begin doing to improve in some area of your life?

chapter 8

Healing Laziness

No one likes to be considered a lazy person. The possibility that any of us might be lazy at crucial times is usually dismissed as untrue or as an outright insult. In spite of the aversion to this term, many of us do far less than we could to use good ideas and our talents or seize good opportunities. We need to consider how poorly we use these factors simply because we fail to act when we could or fail to act forcefully enough to accomplish what is possible.

Laziness is a pejorative term, and we need to keep using it, because it provides a sting to stimulate our thinking to be thorough and honest in evaluating our performance.

Physical Laziness as a Faith Killer
Physical laziness is not always obvious. It tends to be disguised as the need to rest and "restore ourself." We tell ourself that we al-

ready do too much and need to recover from our "strenuous exertions." Or we tell ourself that there is nothing more we can do, and so we stop trying.

While it is possible that these interpretations are valid, the honest person needs to be cautious in leaping to these conclusions. More often than not, we are just being indulgent to our desire for comfort and escape from our labors. A small amount of indulgence is harmless, but large and persistent habits of avoiding hard work can be deadly to our well-being and our faith.

Physical laziness is a faith killer because it will leave us with an ever increasing amount of accomplishments that never happen. As we accumulate a list of failures and half-finished projects, we cannot escape noticing we are underachieving in many key areas. As these defeats become more numerous, it is inevitable that we will become more discouraged and our self-esteem will suffer. Despite the vigor of the excuses we use, despair and doubt will begin to rise in us.

There is no question that many issues and challenges of our life cannot be solved or overcome merely by hard work. Failure alone need not be considered a defeat nor must it depress us—*if we have done all we reasonably can to change matters.* This is the critical issue in how physical laziness becomes a faith killer. If we know we truly did not do enough (after reasonable and objective reflection), then something in us will know we committed a major error of omission. We will know that we failed ourself, and so our faith in ourself will decline.

We can protect ourself from the faith killer of physical laziness by challenging ourself about how much comfort and rest we need. Yes, we all need some, *but are we getting solid value for our rest?* Is the cost of our indolence ("rest and comfort") something huge in terms of lost productivity and self-respect? Would we, for instance, do better to add more self-discipline and dedication to our day?

Emotional Laziness as a Faith Killer

Emotional laziness develops for two primary reasons. For some, it arises out of their selfishness. They consider it to be "natural" to be self-indulgent because they place a high priority on their comfort and convenience. Work, struggle, and sacrifices are things to be avoided at all costs. Personal responsibility is regarded as an insult. The logical consequence is laziness and progressive self-absorption.

For the rest of us, emotional laziness is the end stage of exhaustion. That is, it occurs after we have allowed ourself to engage in excessive and persistent worry, grief, resentment, anxiety, and guilt. Eventually, we reach a point where it seems that life is mainly hostile to our welfare, and we grow weary and apathetic. We stop caring because we are too empty to care much about anything. Unless we curb the excesses of this emotional absorption, we will dissipate our vitality in fruitless obsession. Our faith will be feeble at best. At worst, our faith will be aligned to powerful negative factors.

Emotional laziness is a widespread and serious problem. It is rooted in the strong tendencies to be selfish, angry, despondent, and anxious. Therefore, it is not feasible to try to address the management of these major issues fully in this volume.

However, a few suggestions can be given to restore faith in mild cases of emotional laziness. Once more, knowledge and skill are two powerful resources we have to help us. We need to activate our knowledge to recognize and appreciate whatever good there is in our life. This can be the presence of friends to support us, good opportunities we have to be productive and useful, strengths and talents we have to cultivate these opportunities, and even memories of our past successes. In other words, we need to take time to appreciate what is right in our world and view them as blessings that have the power to sustain us through whatever hardship we bear.

If we shift our attention toward the elements of our life that can nourish us and also restrain our tendencies of self-pity, regret, resentment, and despair, we can overcome emotional laziness. This sets the stage for honest enthusiasm for the good that we can legitimately anticipate in each day. This is one of the major formulas for reversing faith fatigue.

Mental Laziness as a Faith Killer

Mental laziness is rarely recognized or discussed, because it is commonly accepted as normal. Yet the evidence for it can be found in those people who are content to get both their information and instructions in what to think from the popular media and friends. It is natural to expect the media to inform us. And we certainly expect our friends and experts to give us advice. But we must do our own thinking! If we do not, we are mentally lazy.

When our curiosity about life and ideas becomes this weak, we are likely to accept prepackaged ideas and practices that may not serve our highest good. Worse, we gradually slip into the habit of not bothering to check new information for accuracy and validity. And still worse, we fail to examine the events of our life for meaning and significance. The status quo of our beliefs can then engulf us; we drift forward on the momentum of old habits of thought and action. At this point, our faith in all good things has been crippled, buried with our past and what we have been.

A sure sign that mental laziness is killing our faith in our good potential occurs when we accept shallow excuses for why we are less than we could be. We make a habit of justifying our inaction and lack progress in terms such as: *"I don't know what to do. It's not my fault. I have done all I can already. I am helpless to do anything more. My situation is hopeless. I am too tired or sick to do anything more."*

Mental laziness also becomes a problem when we begin to engage in wishful thinking or even magical thinking. The fantasy here is rather subtle—not the kind where people sit around wishing that they will win the lottery. More often it is the belief that just knowing what is wrong and what to do about problems is enough to fix them. Or worse, they affirm or visualize the ideal they desire in the hope that this alone will cause it to manifest. While this technique does have a minimal ability to help, it works largely by motivating us to act. It has little to do with building faith.

A more recent form of mental laziness is found in the entitlement mentality. This is likely to be found in people who assume that they have already suffered too much from perceived adversity, and have now chosen to withdraw from further struggles. From now on, they assume the world and most of the people in it "owe them." They then sulk until "it" is delivered to them. This kind of mental laziness kills faith in our strength, talents, opportunities, and initiative.

The worst kind of mental laziness comes from those who claim to be experts in inspiration. They tells us we need to cultivate the "transparent mind" so that we can receive wisdom directly from "higher sources." The transparent mind is merely code for the empty, passive, turned off mind. Supposedly, our ordinary mental activities and inquiries interfere with the lofty inspiration which we seek. Unfortunately, experience indicates that the transparent mind makes us more open to banalities and stupidity than wisdom. Once more, laziness is disguised as something wonderful that it can never be or achieve.

Mental laziness is a faith killer because it turns off our capacity to seek new and better ideas, make sense of what is happening, and check the accuracy and validity of information. These deficiencies leave us dangerously vulnerable to being mired in the status quo of old ideas and beliefs. Without new input and a means to sort through our experiences, we will be handicapped in our ability to grow and change.

The most effective way to overcome mental laziness is to become intensely interested in what works and what does not. Who seems to be successful and who is not—and why? What is it that they know and are doing that make them so successful and fulfilled while others with similar problems are so frustrated?

Curiosity needs to be directed inwardly if we are going to resurrect faith. There are two questions we need to ask ourself to reawaken curiosity about our own experiences and beliefs.

What do we really know for sure?

How do we know that this is true?

If we ask these kinds of questions frequently *and provide honest answers,* then we will be thinking for ourself—not letting others do our thinking for us.

This will rekindle faith in our own awareness and ability to add solid knowledge and skill to our mental household. In turn, these changes will add new zest to our faith in life.

Spiritual Laziness as a Faith Killer

Spiritual laziness comes in two basic types.

The first is when we expect God to do all the work while we just believe and "accept" God's gifts and miracles. The second major type of spiritual laziness occurs when we are concerned mainly about our own salvation and progress. Both are so common and so widely recommended that they are rarely recognized as another form of laziness.

In too many cases, theologians have succumbed to the public's continual desire for whatever is simple, easy, and effortless. It is unfortunately true that there are too many people who are convinced that they need do very little to lead a spiritual life and achieve redemption. They assume all that is required is to believe in the dogma and practice the outer traditions of worship.

Real change and personal transformation require a huge amount of personal effort. We cannot sit back and just "believe and be" the perfect person our Creator designed us to be. God will not do all the work for us any more than He will plant our vegetables and do our gardening for us. God will provide the seed, soil, sun, and rain for us, but we will have to do the rest. The same applies to everything in our life. We can get guidance, but we will have to apply it to solve our own problems. We can receive love from divine sources, but we will have to do our own forgiving. We can receive strength, but we will have to act courageously to do the things only we can do. We are not designed to be spiritual robots or dummies. The genuine spiritual life is an active partnership with the divine aspects of life.

Spiritual laziness is often encouraged by those who claim that we are all saved by the ancient sacrifice of Jesus. His death did it all for us, they claim, and all we need do is believe in Him, and we are saved from everything bad. While it is true that we are all saved from being lost and abandoned, this is not dependent on our faith in Jesus. It is an inherent part of the spiritual endowment we all have—regardless of our religion or lack of it.

However, being saved from stupidity and the earthbound, selfish life is an entirely different matter. Saving ourself from these threats must be worked out on our own—a long and difficult task of purifying our emotions and illuminating the mind. We need to eradicate negativity and limiting ideas and build up key virtues in our character and lifestyle. God will provide the blueprints for this effort and supply the "bricks and mortar," but we have to do all the work of "laying the bricks."

The worst sort of spiritual laziness is a type commonly found in the East: a person who is very devout and earnestly leading a pure life, yet making little effort to help anyone else. Their attention is focused largely on their personal spiritual path, work of purification, and progressive enlightenment. They have little inclination toward charity and service other than kind thoughts and prayer for others. They are so busy surrendering to God and trying to be harmless, that they fail to notice that they have become useless!

Spiritual laziness becomes a faith killer when it encourages this kind of complacency and self-absorption. We can correct these tendencies with some common sense reflection and work.

The first thing to do is to strive for an active and intelligent partnership between our personality and our divine purpose and design. The simplest step we can take in this direction is to seek God as a mentor who will guide and otherwise help us—not do our work for us.

The second thing to do is to share our blessings—whatever they are. If we are wise and experienced in some area of life, we need to share this knowledge with those who need advice. If we are full of love for life and the joy of living, then share this by being encouraging and an uplifting influence to others. If we are wealthy in terms of money, we need to share it in helpful ways. If we are physically strong and able, we can share our physical labor. As we share what we have, we simultaneously support the work of God and draw closer to the ultimate Source of all Life.

Inactivity can be beneficial, but only when we are ceasing to do harm. Most of the time, we need to be more active—not less. As we pick up our struggle and proceed with dignity, compassion, and courage, we eliminate the inertia in our life. We also restore faith in who we are, what we do, and life itself.

Points to Ponder

1. How jealously do you guard your comfort zone and time for rest and recreation? Do you have the right balance of work and play?

2. Are you working your excuse department overtime? Have you lowered your standards just to accommodate failure or mediocrity?

3. Are you waiting for God to fix something in your life? Or are you busy doing all you can to contribute to what you seek?

4. How did you manage some recent setback? Did you conveniently excuse yourself of all responsibility? Was that fair and realistic?

chapter 9

Healing Rationalization

Rationalization is the product of a clever mind that is seeking simple ways to avoid pesky facts and responsibilities. It smooths over our mistakes and failures by soothing our conscience with gentle lies. It can make us seem heroic just for surviving when we could have triumphed. It will help us feel safe when all we accomplished was to avoid accountability. Rationalization makes us appear honest and responsible when all we have done is deny our role in taking advantage of others. It provides ready-made excuses for being indignant and uncooperative. It will validate our insecurity and justify giving up our attempts to succeed. Rationalization lubricates the already slippery conscience.

Rationalization weakens faith by diverting our attention from truth, reason, and accountability. Without the full function of these safeguards, we can easily wrap ourself in serial self-deceptions. This is what kills faith!

Warning Signs of Rationalization

The habit of rationalization is exceptionally vigorous in certain types of people. It is common in those whose hearts and minds are full of insecurities wrapped in a big ego. Such people are very competitive and have sensitive antennae to search continually for hints of criticism. Their need to appear superior is powerful enough to bend logic and shape facts to deceive themselves and—especially—others. Therefore, a strong tendency toward rationalization should be suspected when anyone makes a habit of bragging about mediocre successes as triumphs, yet never mentioning mistakes and failures. If mistakes are too obvious to ignore, they are blamed on the incompetence or malice of others. This type of rationalizer is always able to make a speedy escape from responsibility.

The ordinary garden variety of rationalizer is usually not quite so adept. These are people who are not very successful in life, and they are in desperate need for effective excuses to protect themselves from accountability and humiliation. They need support and approval.

Therefore, no one is supposed to notice how poorly they are performing or how they are unable to cope with the smallest distress—unless these occasions can be used to procure large amounts of sympathy and assistance. Anyone insensitive enough to suggest how they could improve their situation risks being bathed in a shower of scorn with comments such as: *"This isn't my fault. There is nothing I can do."* After this, the only response to these accusations is a sincere apology and an extra gallon of sympathy.

Rationalization is also the constant companion of perpetually suffering victims. These are people who act as if they have been left out too long and have gone all sour and acid on the inside. Because they know they are so much less than they should be, they are full of anger and self-pity. Every day, they fall down and worship their misery as the monument to all the wonderful things in their life that they have lost or never had. If they are prone to chronic hostility and complaining, they will claim, *"This is just the way I am."* Naturally we are to assume it is totally impossible (and unnecessary) for them to be calm and tolerant, apparently because God made them a natural and congenitally grumpy person. When they are habitually anxious or despondent, we receive the same kind of explanation.

If we are so rude as to suggest gently that they might be overdoing things just very slightly, we will be scolded and reminded that, "You just don't understand the awful things that have happened to me. Anyone in my shoes would act the same way as I have." Once again, we are supposed to accept that having a screaming fit and hitting people is acceptable if we are under stress. In other cases, we are expected to accept a month long pout and sulk as a completely normal response to being told they have to work as hard as others.

Finally, there are emotionally dizzy people who have been in touch with their feelings so long that they have lost touch with both reason and reality. Their god has become whatever makes them feel good. They use good feelings to test the truth and worth of any idea or event. Whatever they feel good about *is* good. Whatever they feel bad about *is* bad. Feeling good is their goal and reward. Avoiding anything that feels bad is their most important priority.

To avoid appearing childish and vain, it is vitally important to find some cover for this childish behavior. Their rescue comes in some of the most brilliant rationalizations of the last hundred years. Suddenly, their special feelings are no longer merely a muddle of assorted fears, cravings, and desires. Now they have been renamed as intuitive guidance that originates in the highest and noblest sources. And who are we to dare to challenge their inspiration—let alone God?

These kinds of rationalizations are faith killers because they create false direction and protect errors. They place large areas of our life in jeopardy of self-deception.

Why We Are Tempted To Rationalize

No one likes to fail or be wrong. No one enjoys mistakes and losses. No one would choose, if given the option, to sabotage his or her health or life activities. Yet these things occur. No one really enjoys being frustrated, anxious, or depressed most of the time, yet many suffer from these chronic moods.

Thus it is we have strong incentives to find new reasons to justify all of these unfortunate conditions. And so we find some way to coat the truth with layers of explanations or denial that leave us faultless. Our humiliation and sense of shame has seized control of parts of our life and placed egotism in control. Thereafter, the truth is sliced and diced and mixed with the oil of rationalization to disguise us as a victim of hostile forces and events.

Unfortunately, the net result is that we may be able to proclaim our innocence, but we will still appear weak, sick, and incompetent. Once more, rationalization can rush to our rescue to make all things wonderful. However, this cover-up requires us to parade our wounds and suffering, so that others can notice them and reward us with extra indulgences and a permanent license to avoid adult standards and responsibilities.

At this point, the work of rationalization has reached its apex. All immaturity, illness, and inadequacies are not merely justified, they have become a badge of honor and a permit to exploit the goodwill and charity of everyone.

Unfortunately, this is a state of addiction to sympathetic attention and support. It is also a first-class case of successful parasitism.

There are many cases of legitimate suffering and illness that represent honest losses of self-sufficiency. No one should deny these people our sympathy and support. However, it is important to be discerning about the credentials of those who claim hardship and loss of ability. Too many exaggerate their distress or prolong it, even though they could overcome it. These people abuse our charity—and expect us to let them continue to do so! We should not permit this kind of rationalization in ourself either.

Clearly, issues of egotism and intellectual dishonesty are key factors in developing and maintaining destructive rationalizations. Unless we get control of these factors, we will have grave difficulty in combating faith fatigue.

Healing Rationalizations

The management of excessive rationalizations begins as we comprehend what makes us vulnerable to using them. If we recognize these factors, the logical course will be to develop the strengths and skills that will neutralize these vulnerabilities.

The gaps in our armor that make us vulnerable to excusing ourself of accountability are a fear of the truth (when it is unfavorable to us), fear of humiliation (by having to admit we were wrong), and a fear of a loss of comfort (by being forced to practice personal responsibility).

The solution to the practice of rationalization is not just to acquire more courage. On the contrary, we need to build up skills and virtues that counter our fears and temptations. This is a difficult task, but worth every moment of the struggle. We need to recognize that we are slowly being trapped in mediocrity, sickness, and suffering.

The key to overcoming the habit of rationalization lies in a major shift of values and priorities. We need to dispose of the great god of comfort and convenience in our life and replace it with the new "god" of truth and integrity. We need to learn how to approach this ideal with commitment, devotion, and determination. Instead of putting our effort into *avoiding* accountability for our life, we need to put it into *accepting* responsibility for our life. If we can take this first step, the rest of the work will become possible.

Beginning with this commitment, we then need to motivate ourself to keep it. We start by reviewing the quality of comfort we are preserving with these rationalizations. We need to ask: *Is it worth it?* In this way, we challenge the value of indulgences and benefits we receive by staying weak, sick, and victimized. How much do they confine us to mediocrity? How often do they make us dependent on the uncertain support and protection from others? How does our demand for constant comfort preclude our potential for the far greater joy of self-sufficiency and productivity. How much does the preservation of our indulgences prevent us from liberating our humanity and soul? Are we paying too high of a price to stay the way we are? Are we ready for change yet?

If we stir up our curiosity by asking these challenging questions, we are likely to remove the blinders to our deceptions. We can then recognize the deeper truth about our potential for greatness and the way for this transformation to occur.

The goal is, naturally, not instant perfection. It is not even eventual perfection. The goal is to *make progress* at being more accountable and self-sufficient at every level: physical, emotional, mental, and spiritual. If we can conceive of these changes, we can then anticipate the worthiness of our struggle to give up the gentle (and not so gentle) lies we have been telling ourself. We can also find the courage to work in earnest to "move ahead" in our life.

This work must be brutally proactive and exclude the poisons of self-pity, endless recriminations, and fear of failure. Strict psychological pragmatism will be essential. We cannot afford to look backward to memories of misery. Nor can we continue to blame the past. Instead, we must start where we are in life now and work every moment to build our future.

If we do this the majority of our time, we will stay committed to truth and act with integrity and allegiance to the best in us and life—including our divine opportunities. In this manner, we live a life governed by principle rather than expedience.

Points to Ponder
1. How often have you considered yourself

to be an innocent victim of unpleasant circumstances? Why have you decided to stay that way?

2. Do you often reject certain ideas or suggestions because they "give you a bad feeling?" Do you realize that the truth about you is often unflattering?

3. Which is worse: the fact of our failure or the fact that we have denied it?

4. How important is personal integrity in your life?

Part Three:
CULTIVATING FAITH BUILDERS

chapter 10

Tools of Faith Building

Once we understand how the major faith killers work to undermine us, we are ready to turn to the work of healing faith fatigue. Just as there are specific attitudes and habits that diminish faith, there are also qualities that repair and increase our faith. These are the "tools" of faith building.

Every builder has the tools of his or her trade. The sculptor of stone has chisels and hammers to create statues. An artist has paints, canvas, and brushes to create works of art. The person who seeks to build faith has wisdom, hope, trust, and courage as tools for this effort. These are the major—but not only—weapons we have to restore faith and neutralize doubt, ignorance, laziness, and rationalization.

A clear understanding of the nature and operation of each of these qualities will prepare us to use them to transform our attitudes. Obviously, none of these qualities is unfamiliar to us. However, until we understand the unique power of each of these forces, we may not be able to harness them fully for the work in faith building.

The Faith Builder of Wisdom

Knowledge is acquired by collecting ideas. Wisdom is acquired mainly by the effort to be productive in *applying* knowledge in our life experience. In other words, wisdom develops as we test and validate or disprove ideas by our experience. It is only by this means that we can be certain about what works and what does not, what endures and what fails in time. Knowledge can inform us about details, but wisdom will bring us comprehension of what these details mean. The knowledgeable person studies the phenomena of life. The wise person knows their origins, relationships, and destiny.

The foundation of our wisdom, therefore, begins with study, observation and the exploration of new mental territories for us. It builds as we gain experience in using these concepts and practices. Only through our own experience can we test them, discarding what is unworthy, and using the rest.

Where this process breaks down is in the

tendency of some people to restrict their study and experiences to familiar and favorable territories. In other words, they read books and study authorities who reflect and support their current beliefs and lifestyle. This is not learning. It is mere repetition and reinforcement of preferred ideas and practices.

The most common reason why people avoid truth and stay stuck in ignorance is that they refuse to look outside their usual sources of guidance. In fact, many give up looking for new ideas and seek only validation of what they already know and do. We cannot grow in wisdom or effectiveness in such a constricted manner.

We need to study what happens to us as well as others. In particular, we need to be extremely curious about those who seem so successful in managing their opportunities and challenges—whatever they are. We need to do more than admire their expertise. We need to discover what they know and what they are doing that makes them so successful! And we should be prepared to discover that luck has very little to do with enduring success and achievement.

There is one basic requirement for this process. That is the need for total and unrelenting intellectual honesty. We are not just seeking to prove that we are right and everyone else is wrong. We are seeking to discern knowledge that is valid, effective, and useful.

Care should be taken that we do not prejudice our search by using self-serving criteria to test the truth. In particular, we need to avoid judging an idea on the basis of whether or not it is popular or if it feels good to us. As a gentle reminder of the falsity of these standards, we should recall that most people in the twelfth century believed the earth was flat. And ordinary alcoholics get "a good feeling" every time they renew their acquaintance with their favorite booze. Common sense—if we use it—will protect us from such nonsense. When we test our ideas and techniques in our own experience and evaluate the long range results, then we will discern what is wise and what is foolish.

Wisdom builds faith by helping us discover and test whatever is a reliable source of guidance, power, and support. It also aids us by validating the techniques we need to use to be productive and effective.

The Faith Builder of Hope

Hope can be defined as the capacity to maintain a steady vision of wonderful possibilities. It is the ability to believe in the presence and potential of many good things in spite of the evidence of imperfection, the fact of opposition, and the presence of criticism. Hope is the consequence of applying wisdom to our life—not wishful thinking or fantasy.

Wisdom is supported by the concepts, values, and principles we have tested and found worthy. Hope is supported by the evidence in our experience that these qualities and powers are sustainable—either by our own efforts or by intangible, archetypal forces. Therefore, they will be available to support us in everything we attempt. In other words, we know what we believe in.

In a more general sense, hope is the essence of the conviction that, in some mysterious way, we are supported by both visible and invisible forces and laws. This need not be a supernatural or esoteric belief. The laws of aerodynamics are invisible and intangible, yet they support every aircraft and bird that flies. The evidence of powerful, intangible forces in our life is massive and frequent.

Hope is always positive. While we can have faith in disaster, hope is always invested in the constructive aspects of life. Therefore, hope helps us build faith by keeping us aligned to our good possibilities.

The Faith Builder of Trust

Trust is based on both wisdom and hope. With wisdom, we validate reliable sources of power and guidance. With hope, we recognize how they have valuable potential uses in many aspects of our life. Trust is the quality that *internalizes* this understanding as a part of our beliefs and habits. In other words, trust harnesses abstract and theoretical possibilities to concrete knowledge, skills, and expectations.

In general, we hope for good possibilities we have not yet literally achieved, but we can trust in the talents and opportunities we have to generate those achievements. For instance, we might hope that we can pass a test, but we can trust that we will after we have prepared for it. Or we hope that we can make good choices and decisions, but we will trust that we can after we have done so several times.

Trust plays a vital role in activating our connection to sources of power, guidance, and other qualities. Hope can prepare our thoughts and beliefs for appreciating constructive possibilities, but trust bonds them to our pragmatic planning and the work of implementing these plans. What our hope envisions, our trust activates. Hope connects us to good possibilities. Trust strengthens what abides in us.

Trust builds faith by anchoring us to sources

of power and guidance that we need for a successful relationship to both opportunities and our challenges.

The Faith Builder of Courage

Courage is the focused and compelling strength we have to accomplish concrete objectives. Courage differs from desires or wishes by being a product of the will—not our emotions. Its deepest roots arise in our will-to-life, that is, the inner impelling urge to thrive and express ourself. It is the power we can harness to give life to our intelligent plans and activities.

While courage stems from deep within us, it is developed in our character only as we cultivate a focus for its applications. As we develop clear understanding about what experiences mean and what works for us, courage will add intensity to our convictions and discipline to our habits. As we develop clear and intelligent plans, courage helps us to activate them. In practical terms, courage is the power we focus into our convictions and commitment to our duties. In general terms, courage provides the strength that supports high self-esteem in us and confidence in what we believe and do.

Power does not become courage until it is harnessed to wisdom and mature values.

Ignorant people can use power to bully and intimidate. Weak people use power to be stubborn and uncooperative. Devious people use power to manipulate others. Foolish people use power to be reckless. The results are quite different when power is used wisely to honor our responsibilities. Then it becomes the courage to perform our duty as we are able to recognize it.

Courage is the partner of all worthwhile things we do. It enables us to be committed to the principles and plans we trust. It activates our values, beliefs, and noble qualities. Courage is essential to pushing back the frontiers of life and work. Courage has the power to protect and preserve what we know to be correct and important. It is the guardian of our dignity, the keeper of the faith, and the protector of commitment to duty.

Courage builds faith by promoting the active expression of our deepest beliefs and values to be effective and useful in the world.

Wisdom, hope, trust, and courage are the instruments we can use to restore faith and build confidence in who we are, where we are headed, and what we are doing. All four are meant to be used together, either alternately or simultaneously.

Collectively, they help us stay focused in our opportunities for achievement and the activities that bring them into manifestation in all that we are and all that we do.

Points to Ponder

1. What do you really know that is valid and accurate? How do you know this is true?

2. How often do you have faith in things that you hope will not happen?

3. Where do you believe in your abilities and plans but do not trust yourself to do something? What does this say about the quality of your belief?

4. If your convictions could be combined with courage, which attitudes and habits would you change?

chapter 11

Faith in People

Faith does not exist in a vacuum. It does not have a separate existence from us like a shoe that we can send out for repairs. It is part of who we are, what we have done, and what we are doing. While we sometimes refer to specific people as someone who "has faith," we always mean that he or she has faith in *something*. Faith connects us to qualities, authorities, noble ideas, activities, and situations. Consequently, when we say our faith is exhausted, we usually mean our faith in something is faltering. Therefore, our efforts to repair faith fatigue need to be addressed to those relationships that are failing.

The key relationships commonly associated with faith fatigue are our connections to:
1. People, including ourself.
2. Our life situation and experiences.
3. Higher powers and divine opportunities.

These are the major battlegrounds where disappointment, frustration, and exhaustion can overwhelm our ability to sustain faith in constructive elements. For this reason, we need to know how to use the tools of wisdom, hope, trust, and courage effectively to build a healthy connection in each of these areas.

Healthy relationships in these key areas are important because they control the flow of information, love, and power *to* us as well as *from* us. In other words, a large part of what we can be and do depends on the quality of our relationships to people, events, authorities, and opportunities. If we are discouraged and afraid, the relationship we have with our own strengths, skills, and knowledge will be feeble. Our ability to assert ourself will be marginal at best. If our relationships to others, events, and opportunities are poor, we may not be sufficiently guided, loved, and supported. All of these relationships will have a powerful influence on our ability to thrive in the world.

These key relationships are *defined* by the quality of our understanding, attitudes, responsibility, and activities. The *result* of any relationship depends on the degree of rapport and collaboration we can establish with the parties, issues, or forces that are our partners. We have limited—often only minimal—power to control either the definition or the result of any relationship. We rarely have the luxury of dealing with certainties and guarantees. Instead, we must cope with multiple possibilities.

The intelligent use of faith is a priceless ingredient for dealing with possibilities. The force, quality, and persistency of our faith can be the single most important factor in contributing to our success or failure in these three key relationships—with others, with ourself, and with higher powers. If we are to master the work of healing faith fatigue and building mature qualities of faith, we need to know how to use it in these primary relationships.

This is the reason why it is important to understand the basic fact that we do not just have faith, *we have faith in something*. We have faith (or not) in the motives, qualities, and behavior of others. We have faith (or not) in our own abilities, self-control, and endurance. Or we have faith (or not) in the guidance and support of higher powers. Faith fatigue often begins when we misunderstand or distort our perceptions of these connections. If this occurs, we may create multiple generations of distress and confusion.

These principles are easily demonstrated in our relationships with other people. Right relationships that are solid, effective, and enduring are neither established nor cemented with feelings. They are based on shared needs and interests, shared values, responsibilities, problems, activities, and rewards. These are the factors that can be objects of our good faith. We just need to apply wisdom to discovering the best aspects of these factors. If we can find them, then we can add hope to sustain our faith and trust to ground these positive beliefs in our expectations and attitudes. Thereafter, our courage can assist us in acting in ways that honor our faith in the value of the relationship we have with people.

In more concrete terms, faith helps us to find many reasons to respect and support the goodness in ourself and others. Faith will also assist us in finding many reasons to tolerate the annoying aspects of others. More importantly, faith will aid in finding many reasons to respect our own abilities and accomplishments while we gracefully bear our limitations and burdens.

The key here is *right understanding*, which leads to a sensible and balanced view of people and ourself. This is the crux of where faith and respect can break down. If we fail to cultivate a right understanding of others, we can expect faith fatigue to set in rapidly. We will then have to repair one or more of the following problems:

First, we fail to see the good (real or potential) in ourself or others. Usually, this is because we are blinded by the faults we perceive. Almost everyone has a few habits any decent person would find annoying, but most people have many good aspects we can respect, if not admire. If we wait to find all the "right people" (at least as good as we are), it may be a long and fruitless wait. In the meantime, we will miss many opportunities to help and be helped by "imperfect" people.

One reason for this omission is the tendency to accept automatically two false notions. The first is the invalid assumption that people who do not think and act like us are inferior. We all have our strengths and weaknesses. Where we are strong and talented, others may be weak. And where we are not very skillful or knowledgeable, others may be strong. In general, people are just different, and we should be thankful they are. If every vegetable was a bean and every flower was a daisy, it would be a dull and impoverished world. Variety is not only desirable, it is a necessity. The same observation applies to people.

The second reason we damage relationships with people is because we become excessively annoyed and critical about their idiosyncrasies. We may make the shallow judgment that we would make a complete mess of our life if we behaved the way others do. What we forget is that most people are successful in their life, their chosen career, or their marriage precisely because they have those "odd" traits and mannerisms. Thoughtful, detail oriented, fussy people are needed for careers in computer science and accounting. Relaxed, friendly, talkative, emotional types are needed for good public relations. Introverted, studious types are needed for scientific research. Extroverted and passionate types are needed for roles in the entertainment industry. Gentle, sensitive, and nurturing types are needed in the helping professions. Aggressive, confident types are needed for leadership positions.

What we decide is a character flaw or annoying habit may be what others *must* have to be productive and effective in their world. As irritating as it might be to us, we need to grant that their style works for them. If that is a difficult leap of insight to swallow, then we need to consider how difficult or boring it would be if we had to thrive in their job or marriage or other responsibilities. If we imagine ourself "in their shoes," we might trigger a small epiphany of tolerance for who they are and how they behave. We might also understand that other people are often successful *because* of what *we view as an idiosyncrasy—not in spite of it.*

Because of these different temperaments and habits, people have a variety of perspectives, values, and strengths. They usually also have a special way of collecting and processing information and solving problems that works best for them. We often lose faith in people because we fail to adjust ourself to these differences in deciding what is important about a situation or the best way to manage it.

If we look beyond these superficial traits and behavior, we can find elements of goodwill, integrity, accountability, and knowledge that are worth our respect and faith.

We can find many ways to apply the tools of faith building if we consider one more factor that causes the breakdown of relationships with people and parts of ourself. When people fail us or when we fail to meet our own expectations, we can lose faith very rapidly and, sometimes, permanently. No one likes incompetence, dishonesty, laziness, or selfishness. These four characteristics ruin many things. Yet traces of them are so common in parts of ourself and others, that we must find a better way to respond to them than by rejection and condemnation.

The way to begin restoring faith in ourself and others often requires that we comprehend that we are all on a "learning curve." That is, we are all in the process of learning our lessons to become stronger, smarter, more skillful, more assertive, or more patient and self-disciplined. Yes, some people are dense and refuse to learn at all. Yet, most of us become the competent, able, and brilliant people we are exactly because we take on challenges, risk making mistakes, miss opportunities, and learn from all of this. All of our experiences—good and bad, our own and others—can provide the material for the master lessons of life. Experience eventually becomes the great teacher for all.

If we can appreciate this fact when we are disappointed or offended by others, we may be more able to keep the faith in these relationships. It is doubly essential when we begin to condemn *ourself* for errors and lapses of judgment and behavior. Keeping the faith in ourself depends on our conviction that every "mistake" and every "failure" is part of our journey towards self-mastery and mastery of our life situation. If we apply this same wisdom to our analysis of all people, then our hope, trust, and courage can rebuild our faith.

Repairing Faith Fatigue

Our faith often breaks down when relationships with people are afflicted with distrust, competition, alienation, jealousy, malice, and indifference. If we add to this our denial of any good potential and begin expecting the worst, we will enter a downward spiral that cannot be reversed.

The solutions that repair faith fatigue in these areas involve three steps:

First, we need to discover where points of harmony already exist between ourself and others. Very often, these exist at one or two levels deeper than the annoying behavior that consumes our attention. For instance, we may agree on the ultimate purpose and goal of a major project, but disagree about the specific plans for completing it. Or we may agree perfectly about the important principles for raising our children; we only disagree about the details. Or we might all be committed to helping people get off welfare and become self-sufficient, yet disagree on the details of how it can be done most effectively.

This first hurdle can be difficult for people who have great trouble discerning what are fundamental elements and what are merely details. Religion is a common battleground for this problem. Differing religious groups usually share a basic belief in a benevolent Creator who protects life and supports order and justice. The fundamentals of how they worship and serve God are also very similar, i.e., gathering in groups, praying, reading from scriptures, affirming their faith, living a virtuous life, and helping one another. None of these fundamentals should be threatening to most decent people. However, lesser details of these practices seem to become larger than life—or God—in the minds and hearts of certain devotees and theologians. Some of them lose their sense of proportion so that the details become the fundamentals and the fundamentals are lost in the smoke and fire.

Reasonable people, of course, are able to recognize and honor the underlying principles and noble ideas behind all of the phenomena of life. Until we consistently think and act with this understanding, we risk chronic and recurring poor relationships with others and disharmony within ourself. If we can take this basic first step, we are half way to the resolution of conflicts and far along our way to building up our faith in people.

The major value of establishing these points of agreement is that this step removes major adversarial views and attitudes from the primary core of our relationship. Thereafter, it becomes possible to work proactively instead of antagonistically in our efforts to resolve conflicts. This does not guarantee harmony, and loyal support for basic needs and welfare. Dozens of acts of respect are ignored if there are not enough words and adoring glances to go with them. Many a friendship has evaporated when there were insufficient hugs and kisses, despite the presence of encouragement and prolonged support in times of need.

If we establish our bond with others at the level of these petty details, we are doomed to much frustration. We will be missing the mature nourishment that we could be receiving, and we may be forcing our friends and family to relate to us as a child.

However, if we shift our priorities and make the genuine fundamentals of the relationship the basis for our bond, we enter a different world. Now we have far more to share, support, and enjoy than before. We can enjoy each other's presence and contribution. In other words, we have a friend—not an adversary.

This style of rapport can also apply to our relationship with parts of ourself. We may need to work at increasing our harmony with our conscience and department of curiosity and creativity. A part of us may want to break out of our old habits and try new things and be more assertive. Our basic friendliness and eagerness for more socializing may be in conflict with our desire for privacy and fear of rejection. If we review the nature of our basic values and principles, we can start anew in sorting out the details of how we are going to express our creativity, curiosity, and assertiveness in a fair and balanced manner. The details of what and how we will do this will fall into place, but only if we first set out the larger context of our lifestyle.

The third and final step comes as we trust ourself and our insights enough to let them control our behavior. This can be the most difficult step of all. Many people find that the difference between knowing what to do and doing it is a chasm of immense width. They may not think of it that way, but they act that way. The reason seems to be the force of old habits and the natural fear of risk that comes with any change.

Now is when we need to exercise every one of the four major tools of faith building. We need to review the wisdom of concentrating on the deeper and fundamental value of our relationship and the factors that already bond us to others or bind our own life together. As we reflect on these issues, we can generate a strong hope that these factors are powerful and enduring enough to transcend our differences. As these realizations build up in us, we come to trust enough in our own judgment and perspective to have the courage to change our behavior. This is the basic formula for repairing faith in our relationships to others and the broken parts in us.

In these ways we can begin to act as if almost everyone has value and is worthy of our interest and support. And even more importantly, we will become more centered in our core values, noble qualities, and wisdom. This will repair many things in ourself in addition to our dignity and our faith in what we do.

The work of building faith in people depends on two highly significant principles. First, whether we recognize it or not, we are our brothers and sisters keepers. The question has been posed for dozens of generations, but it was answered a long time ago. The second principle is that the helping hand we seek is at the end of our own arm.

These simple thoughts are neither new nor unclear. When we come to accept these truths as fundamental principles of our life, we will have enormously strengthened our ability to fight faith fatigue.

Points To Ponder

1. Do you have much faith in your ability to manage stress? Why not?

2. Why do you need key people in your life? Where do you share values, needs, work, and rewards?

3. What is the quality of your "sharing" with them?

4. Where can you improve harmony within yourself?

chapter 12

Faith in Our Experiences

The accepted wisdom is that experience is what makes us who we are. This is the basic precept of psychologists and sociologists who assume our fundamental sense of identity, core values, and major beliefs are determined by the type of experiences we have. In short, the influence of parents, peers, and other authority figures shape our beliefs. Our culture sets the tone of our primary values and outlook on life. Our friends and happy experiences build our self-esteem and strengthen our good characteristics. Our enemies and the adversity we endure diminish our joy in living and weaken us. Thereafter, the tone and quality of our life and self-expression is relatively fixed. All that is left to us is to adjust to who we are and what has happened.

The problem with this picture is that it is wrong and terribly misleading. The popularity of this interpretation of life, while enormous, does not make it right.

The difficulty in comprehending this challenge to the common wisdom is that it is sometimes true—for those who have chosen to act like robots and sleepwalk through their lives. Billions of people have unwittingly made this choice without even being aware that they have made any choice at all. None of them appear catatonic or drugged. Most of them have busy lives, careers, and children. They are active in the professions and take on leadership positions in society. Many of them may well be close friends and family members. But they are enthralled by the traditions and habits (good or bad) of mass consciousness. They rarely consider acting outside of the range of accepted thought and behaviors of their group. Any significant loss causes them to be discouraged and feel defeated. Any significant insult or threat causes them to be resentful and feel hostile. Any major challenge causes them to be anxious and feel afraid. In this sense, they *are* robots. These people are not fully aware that they can—at any moment—wake up and realize three important facts. As adults, we all have the power to acquire and fully comprehend these elments of wisdom. The first fact is that we will all experience some measure of loss, failure, resistance, rejection, and conflict. We will not be able to avoid some variety of these events. The second fact is that what is happening—or has happened—to us is less important than how we choose to respond to it. The third is the fact that we do have some choices in how we respond to these issues. None of these three ideas is new, but understanding them is rare—and hardly ever used as a basis for mature living or healing our problems.

The significance of these ideas is extremely important to our work of repairing faith fatigue. Recall that faith is our most powerful tool in our initial work with *any* possibility—whether it is for success or defeat. Our faith in our possibilities of success summons our strengths and charges our activities with the power to assert ourself. Our faith in doom summons all of our self-sabotaging traits and empowers them to take charge of our life. What usually happens after that? The quality and direction of our faith has the potential to make or destroy us.

Thus it is that our ability to have a successful relationship with our experiences—past or present—pivots around the quality of faith in two things: how we interpret the meaning of these experiences, and how we choose to respond to them. Both of these are choices we can make. We just need to make these decisions with as much wisdom and courage as possible.

Building a Bond with Wisdom and Hope

The first bit of wisdom that will confront us when we wake up and cease to sleepwalk through life is the realization that we are always more than our experiences. This is not just a nice philosophical concept for idle speculation. It is solid fact for those bold enough to embrace it. Yes, of course we experience many failures and successes, losses and gains. We miss some opportunities and connect with others. We have our moments of bliss as well as disappointment. But amidst all of this huge variety of experiences, something about us remains apart from them. This part of us is able to observe, speculate, interpret, imagine, decide what to do, and choose when to act. It does not feel—it understands what our feelings mean. It does not see or hear—it determines the usefulness and validity of what we see and hear. It does not act—it decides what to do if we should act. It does not react to what happens—it chooses the response, if any. People who are awake and have left the robot stage do these things all the time.

Psychologists refer to this as focusing our attention in the observing self rather than the reactive self. The difference is huge, because it determines whether or not we are able to take charge of our life or continue as a programmed robot. Our reactive self (our outer awareness) is usually possessed by the immediate sensations of what is seen, heard, and felt—both physically and emotionally. The observing self, however, is able to connect with all of our strengths and virtues. It can draw on them to interpret our outer circumstances and sensations as well as associated memories. By being awake and centering our attention in our observing self, we are far more aware of our higher possibilities. In this way, we can nourish our faith as well as other strengths useful to reversing our faith fatigue.

The second aspect of wisdom that helps us build up a constructive faith in the value of all of our experiences stems from the "discovery" of the universal laws that govern human behavior. The fact that there are such laws is not subject to debate. Their impact does not depend on either our awareness of them or our belief in them.

If we doubt that such laws exist and influence us without our permission, we need to remember that water can drown a stupid person as easily as an intelligent one. The potent influence of these laws becomes apparent with careful examination of human experience. Prejudiced and ignorant people will not find this evidence, but then deaf people do not hear music either—despite the fact that music exists.

The first law that awake and aware people need in order to restore faith in the value of their experiences is the Law of Externalization. This law guarantees that our "true colors" cannot be concealed; they will show themselves in what we do and say and how and when we do it. This means our basic hostility will be apparent and intrude on our behavior in spite of our attempts to be polite. Our shyness will inhibit our speech in spite of any attempt we make to cover it up with gregariousness. And our ignorance will limit our perceptions and our responses, in spite of efforts to cooperate. What we are internally, *as a personality,* will dominate our self expression.

This means a shallow effort to improve our *style* will prove ineffective in time. Polite manners and a polished act are useful and valuable, but they are no substitute for effective change. They affect only style and appearance without modifying our core character traits. In other words, a mask for our dishonesty and rudeness will not turn us into a saintly person. All it will do is fool a few people part of the time while the habit of deceit and boorishness continues unabated. In the meantime, discerning people will penetrate the mask and recognize the truth about matters.

The major signficance of the Law of Externalization is that it works in our favor to help us transform ourself and what we do. Through these changes, we can make great strides in building up our faith in the value of our experiences.

Just as the force of the law gravity can work for or against us, the Law of Externalization will help us as often as it harms us. It all depends on what we have inside of us to be externalized or manifested. This means the sincere person who truly cares for people and has enduring compassion will show it and keep showing it long after the huggers and glad handers have exhausted their tiny stores of goodwill. In times of real need, the sincere person will provide care, while the phonies hide out. In times of hardship and stress, he will be digging in to hold things together and to do what good he can, while the shallow will have long given up and gone home. Real virtue shows. Genuine intelligence and creativity will be apparent. A sincere love of life and joy in being will not quit in tough times.

The healing and transforming potential of

but it does create a climate in which we have identified fundamental values, purposes, goals, and principles that can be the foundation for both the relationship and our efforts to rebuild our faith. We now can keep faith in the clearly identified constructive elements of this relationship—not just obsess about our problems.

The second step we need to take to build up faith in our relationships is to bond to others at these points of shared interests, qualities, opportunities, needs, and rewards. Even if we find there are only a few of these elements, we need to let them dominate our relationship. Whatever disharmony exists is then contained in a larger context of shared values and mutual respect.

It is tragic that the bulk of friction among individuals and groups is usually focused on the small and most petty details. Religious fanatics, for instance, focus more on their favored prophet than in the God the prophet served. Championing minor dogma and focusing on tradition becomes more important than acts of charity and kindness. Being loyal to their religious group becomes more important than integrity and basic kindness.

Similar divisions often occur among people. Outer signs of affection and attention (or their lack) can become more important than constant working with the Law of Externalization is huge. Giving up shallow efforts to change our style in favor of major shifts of our values and priorities will lead to significant and enduring change. A sincere compassion for people will nullify the outer resentment we might have for some petty adversary. A deep urge to be effective and productive in the world will nullify our habitual fears and inhibitions.

The secret of using the Law of Externalization to build faith is to work at a deep inner level of our most important values, beliefs, and intentions. If we make sincere changes at this level, they will sweep through the outer layers of our personality.

This conversion is not easy to perform, but the principle behind it is valid. It does not require extraordinary abilities to achieve. Every good actor learns to do it well. Untalented actors merely learn their lines, imitate a few gestures, and learn where to stand. Their performances are tepid and unimpressive, and the audience knows it. But good actors work quite differently. If they are to play the part of a tyrant, they pull out their resources of aggressiveness and malice to be convincing in the role. If they are to play the role of a seducer, they will draw on their deep resources of desire and charm. And when they play the part of a great leader, they must draw forth their capacity for authority, decision, and self-confidence.

Centuries of successful actors have proven that this technique works very well. The Law of Externalizations will work for us just as well. We can use it to develop greater faith in both the value and meaning of our experiences and our ability to take charge of our life.

The second universal law that we can utilize to build faith and better relationships with our experiences is the Law of Response. This Law states that our life situation will respond in a manner that is similar to what we send out to it. The other way to describe the action of this Law is to state that everything we do will have consequences that reflect the quality of our act. For instance, our words and deeds of anger will stimulate a response along similar lines. Our words and deeds of charity will invoke a charitable response from somewhere.

The simplest way to understand this law is to appreciate that life, and the people in it, will treat us about as well as we treat them. If we are mean, devious, greedy, and destructive, this is what we will harvest. If we are kind, helpful, and honest, we will harvest the effects of these traits. In the Bible, this law is referred to in the famous line: *"As you sow, so you reap!"*

All of this has enormous significance in our

effort to repair our capacity for faith and build faith in the value of our experiences. If we comprehend the impact of this law, it means that there is a powerful message in what *habitually* happens to us. The unpleasant outer events we have blamed for our discouragement, anxiety, or anger may not be the reason we feel that way at all. They may be the *consequences* of years of being too liberal in expressing our grumpiness, intimidation, and condemnation. These unpleasant events *may* also be the indirect consequences of the usual quality of our thoughts, expectations, judgments, and what we have said and done or left undone.

If we find any truth in this realization, we owe it to ourself to launch a major review of how we have interpreted many major events in our life and what we need to change in our beliefs and behavior.

Fortunately, the positive side of this Law works very much in our favor when we seek to build faith and transform the quality of our convictions and attitudes. If we make sincere efforts to invest our joy, compassion, charity, integrity, and wisdom into everything we do, our life experience will inevitably change. This change may not occur instantly or in every case. But the broad trends and momentum of our life experiences will gradually change as we change ourself and our self-expression. This will not occur because we wish it could happen. It will occur because it is the law!

If we arm ourself with a full understanding of these Laws, our thinking will be more aligned to constructive possibilities. This, in turn, will generate a strong and enduring hope in many wonderful prospects for ourself. Recall that hope is the capacity to sustain a constructive vision of our strengths, talents, and the wonderful things we can achieve with them. Wisdom feeds our hope, and our hope will guide and nourish a new and stronger faith in the value of all of our experiences—good, bad, or mediocre.

Building a Relation with Trust and Courage

There is an old saying that knowledge is power. We can convert wisdom to power as we trust in our firm conviction that something within us is stronger and more powerful than any distress we have about our experiences. This will empower us to take greater charge of our life. As we learn to convert wisdom to personal power, we come to understand the importance of conforming our thinking and behavior to the action of divine law. This change will make the universe our ally, instead of our enemy.

Just knowing of these possibilites is not enough. We must think and act with these insights. Our wisdom and hope of taking charge of our life can nourish the internalization of this information until we trust it enough to act on it. There is an abundance of possibilities worthy of our faith, but we will have to cultivate them with our respect and determination to make them the centerpiece of our life.

An important step from victim to the director of our experiences is to cultivate a new sense of who we are. We need to accept all of our experiences in a new light. This new view is that we are more than our experiences, good or bad; we are the interpreter and harvester of everything that happens to us.

That is, we have a new role of sorting and sifting through our experiences and extracting the meaning, lessons, skills, and virtues acquired in them. We are no longer a victim of events, even though bad things that we cannot prevent may still continue to happen. A victim just lets life happen. But those who impose their ability to choose their response to what happens liberate themselves from victim status.

If we work with this understanding and trust ourself to maintain this perspective, we will have many opportunities to develop a whole new relationship to our experiences. This includes even those old experiences we assumed would forever shape our fears, resentments, and regrets. It also includes all of our beliefs about what we cannot do or have.

By trusting in our knowledge, skill, and universal law, we can liberate new and better dimensions of our humanity and new degrees of accomplishment in our life.

We should always keep in mind that we are all still learning our master lessons to be more wise, virtuous, and successful. As we view our experiences in this light, they become bountiful fields in which we harvest the knowledge, qualities, and skills that build virtue and self-mastery.

This is how we build greater faith in our experiences.

The events of our life can wear us down or not depending on how we respond to them. If we allow our automatic reactions of resentment, fear, and sadness to take over, we will be doomed to recurring bouts of frustration and limited accomplishment. We need to be as creative and innovative as possible in order to manifest a healthy response to what happens to us. More importantly, we need to take charge of how we interpret and respond to our experiences.

Life is an adventure to be lived—not a burden to be endured. That is why we are all given a figurative map and compass to find and explore our many opportunities to grow and thrive. When we stop approaching life as a spectator event, we learn how to transform experience into rich opportunity.

Points To Ponder

1. Do you see yourself mainly as a product of experiences you did not control? Or are you mainly a product of your own choices? Is it time to take more charge of your life?

2. How often do you take time to appreciate how you have grown and become stronger precisely because you have endured hardships?

3. Do you understand how life usually treats you about as well as you treat it? Are you sure?

4. Do you know when to streamline your life and stop being so concerned about things you cannot change?

chapter 13

Faith in Divine Opportunity

The fundamental fact about our humanity is that our nature and life is rooted in spirit. From these origins, we derive many innate resources, a design for maturity, a plan for its manifestation, and the impelling urge to grow and be useful in the world. This is true for ourself as well as others. All people have their origins in the same universal life force, and all of them are endowed with their own inner resources and unique design for mature living.

Our inner life of divine possibilities is a great resource for healing, renewal and enrichment. It is tragic that so few have learned to use it effectively. It is even worse that many do not believe this resource is available to them. Most of this problem is due to ignorance. Some is due to bad religion that has misdirected people to the mere idolization of spirit.

Healing our faith fatigue, as well as a myriad

of others problems, is difficult—if not impossible—without a collaborative relationship with our divine possibilities. These are the wellsprings of all of our strengths, wisdom, talents, joy, health, and capacity for useful self-expression. Whether we accept the fact or not, we ultimately depend on these inner powers for our well-being. We need to know how to establish and strengthen our attunement to these sources of humanitarian strength.

Believing in these resources is a beginning point, but hardly enough to make us fully receptive to their benefits. Before we add to our faith or begin new work to tap into our inner life, we need wisdom. We need to know more about our inner nature and our innate resources of wisdom, love, power, talent, self-control, and love. This understanding can then provide a new focus for our faith and a nucleus for our work of healing faith fatigue.

The Apostle Paul demonstrated in his life a profound wisdom about faith in action. He often mentioned that his faith helped him overcome tremendous hardship, suffering, and the ferocious attacks he endured. While his letters describe in detail what he believed in and what he did, the best single description of *how* he sustained his faith was when we wrote: "I believe, but I know what I believe in." In other words, his belief was anchored in a source of power and authority that tangibly supported and protected him. These deep convictions added courage to his strength, guidance to his understanding, joy to his enthusiasm, stamina to his patience, and force to his self-control.

We, too, need to know what we believe in so that we can draw strength to support our convictions, confidence to help us believe in ourself, and courage to sustain what we would do.

Fortunately, this wisdom need not be totally esoteric or arcane. To heal our faith fatigue, we simply need to be clear about our foundation and our priorities so we can separate ourself from the clutter in our life, past or present.

Our Foundation in the Life of Spirit

Our foundation is not the body, our feelings, or any particular set of experiences. Our foundation lies in the deepest sources of our life force and the inner design we have for greatness. It is not necessary to understand completely the origins of this in order to rely on it and use it for guidance and strength. This foundation has many names—but the names matter little.

The nature of this foundation is described best in terms of its impact on the quality of our life. It is what endures in times of sickness and despair. It is what is unchanged by adulation and flattery. It is what remains after our triumphs and failures. It is the innate storehouse of our treasures of consciousness and design for right living that is revealed to us throughout our life experience. It precedes our physical birth as well as survives death, because it transcends all earthly experiences—even if we do not currently believe this. It is the core of our being. Shallow people do not recognize it. Phony people are threatened by it. Cynical people scoff at it. Yet it prevails as the nucleus of who we are.

This is the source of strength we can always rely on in time of need. It is a potent force for building faith.

Developing the Link to Our Foundation

This powerhouse of wisdom and other virtues does not emerge spontaneously in our life. It *never* appears because we are empty and obedient. The treasures of our divine resources come to us because we have created enlightened beliefs and abilities in our character as a vehicle for these great potentials.

Instead of destroying the ego and just getting ourself out of the way (as many misguided theologians advocate), we need to develop and purify the personality. It is the best of our personal knowledge, skills, compassion, courage (and all other fruits of the spirit) that become a bridge to divine possibilities.

As we build a core of enlightened qualities in our personality, we also need to cultivate enlightened priorities to focus the best in us on our divine potentials. As long as our desires are directed primarily to satisfy our wish for personal comfort and convenience, we will stay relatively earthbound. It is our enlightened priorities that open the figurative door to our noble foundation of core strengths and virtues.

Unfortunately, many people define what is most important for them by imitating whatever is popular in mass consciousness. They base their priorities on what is pleasant, convenient, or expedient. If we are to have correct and effective priorities, we need to draw them from our deepest humanitarian values and purposes—the foundation of our life. Only these will give skillful direction to the power we have.

Activating our Divine Potential

The great plan for all of humanity requires that we must activate our deeper potential for knowledge, skills, and virtues through our life experiences. Mere academic study about forgiveness or faith will not be enough. Neither will we be "given" these virtues in some mysterious fashion. What remains is the necessity to develop them through our own struggles of trial and error.

While many people will not accept it as a fact of life, our conduct is governed by Universal Law. In particular, our progress is guided by the Law of Establishing Harmony out of Conflict. In other words, significant growth of our wisdom, skill, compassion, courage or others virtues will come from our successful involvement with major challenges and hardships. It is our struggle with these which compel us to activate our capacity to be creative, skillful, tolerant, forgiving, and steadfast. As we acquire new degrees of these virtues, we are released from our suffering.

This concept is vital to our ability to cultivate a strong faith in our divine opportunities. It means that we need to understand why we must cease to resent or fear our hardships and struggles, as difficult as this act may be for us. No one enjoys problems or the misery they bring, and we are not expected to want more than we have. However, the mature person needs to keep faith that there is a certain reward that will come as we cope successfully with whatever challenges us.

The pragmatic significance of this concept is profound. It means that no legitimate suffering is ever in vain, and no great loss is without some compensation for us. This reward or compensation might be new abilities, self-control, or joy. At the very least, it can be the absolute conviction that we are stronger and more resourceful than we ever believed we could become. Because of this, we can thereafter face our future with far more confidence and inner peace than we have ever known before.

New Opportunities and Directions

Faith fatigue is a chronic and recurring problem for many people. Just because we may survive a crisis or two will not make us immune to new challenges. We may well be stronger and smarter because of how well we have handled previous experiences, but there is always more to learn. We need to be ready for new challenges. This means there will be new opportunities for discouragement and frustration and the possible erosion of our faith. For this reason, we need to keep faith in the fact that there is a powerful and valid reason for our involvement in these new challenges as well as inner power to conquer them.

The issue of personal growth and our divine design is complex and subtle. Outer events and demands are not the only forces that direct our life experience. While new opportunities or demands seize our outer attention, our inner self also has its own plans and priorities. This is because our inner self is continually seeking to express its purpose in our character and lifestyle.

Because of this fact, we may find that something deep within us can withdraw its interest in supporting our personality's old beliefs, habits, and activities—if it has not done so long ago. It is as though something in us is moving on and we need to move with it. In other words, our inner design and plan is unfolding, seeking to carry us into new adventures and relationships with life.

Our response to this may be a loss of enthusiasm or interest in what used to be exciting and challenging. This is the most subtle type of faith fatigue that we can experience. If we are effectively aligned to our inner life, we will recognize the call of spirit to new directions and respond appropriately. We need to be open to the possibility that this may be happening to us from time to time.

Hope Links Us to Faith

As we come to comprehend our inner nature and its need to act in accordance with Universal Law, we will begin to see through the fog of our personality's confusion and distress. Our priorities begin to shift away from seeking the fulfillment of every wish and trying escape from every unpleasantness. With wisdom, comes the vision to understand what is our highest good and the need to pursue it. Wisdom opens our capacity to develop a steady hope of good potential everywhere—especially in ourself.

In particular, our hope will align us to a solid faith that there is, somehow, a fulfilling life beyond—or in spite of—our distress and disappointment. As we decide to live our life this way, we will inevitably acquire the experiences that validate for us the fact that there are intelligent and benevolent forces at play in our life. Our understanding of these things may be partial, but we will be able to have faith that there is an Intelligence and Power available to us that is far greater than our personality's wishes, fears, or distress.

By learning to follow the guidance of this less chosen path we will be lead to many adventures and rewards. In these ways, we will add to our capacity to trust in our internal powers, qualities, and direction. In doing so, we summon the courage to act this way in all that we are and all that we do.

As we think and act in this manner, we activate our inner life as a continual source of inspiration and support for all worthwhile endeavors. Right thought, belief, and action will bring into play an infinite source of benevolent Intelligence *that has faith in us.* This is the ultimate and most powerful way to heal faith fatigue and build the strong and intelligent use of faith.

Points to Ponder

1. What do you believe are your most useful sources of guidance and strength? Are they available and reliable?

2. What have you used as the foundation for your beliefs and lifestyle? What standards do you use to set your priorities?

3. Do you really believe that there is a good quality of life after loss and suffering? If so, are there a few attitudes you need to change?

4. Even if your patience and self-control are weaker than your frustration and anger, do you still trust in the *value* of patience and self-control? If not, why not?

Conclusion

Our human nature is continually prone to various temptations such as resentment, self-pity, anxiety, doubt, and the desire to seek instant comfort. The mixtures and strengths of these faith killers—and the experiences that trigger them—occur with many variations. Some people are more prone to setbacks in certain periods of their life. Others are more vulnerable to recurring faith killers, such as depression or anxiety. Just when we think we have mastered one of these killers, they come rushing back—perhaps from a new direction or in a new disguise. But they do tend to return.

If we are thoroughly grounded in the signs of faith fatigue and knowledge of how to manage it, we can control the damage before it takes root in our lives and grows to significant dimensions once more. Therefore, it will be useful to review the principles of managing faith fatigue with some regularity. Not only will we strengthen our ability to combat faith fatigue, but the same principles and techniques will also summon the best in us and help us in the process of personal transformation in many other areas.

Remember, health—including psychological and spiritual health—is much more than just not being sick, worried, sad, resentful, or confused and uncertain. The repair of faith needs to be complemented with an increase in all our virtues.

May this be your destiny.

Want More?

Additional copies of *Faith Fatigue* can be purchased at your favorite bookstore or directly from the publisher, Enthea Press, P.O. Box 251, Marble Hill, GA 30148. Please send $20 for each copy, plus $6 for shipping for one copy; $8 postage for two or more copies. On orders of 10 or more copies, the cost per book will be $14, plus postage.

You may also order by internet and pay for the order by PayPal. Our e-mail address is lig201@lightariel.com. The Enthea Press web site is www.lightariel.com.

The following books by Robert R. Leichtman, M.D. (and more) may also be bought in the same way:

FEAR NO EVIL
Using the 23rd Psalm for Healing.

PSYCHIC SELF-DESTRUCTION
And How To Reverse It.

THE PSYCHIC LIFE
Seeing Beyond the Mundane.

PSYCHIC VANDALISM
Preventing it From Ruining Our Lives.